The Sufferings of the Nathan Soul

In meiner Aura
   schaue ich
mit Michaels Auge
mit Christi Kraft
mit Weihemacht:
   Wie waltet
      In mir
   Göttlich=Geistiges.

Göttlich=geistiges
Von obern Weltenorten
Durchstrahlet es mich;

Göttlich=geistiges
Aus weitem Welten-Umkreis
Durchwellet es mich.

Göttlich=geistiges
Aus tiefen Erdenklüften
Durchströmet es mich.

Die Sterne
von oben
tragen Göttlich=Geistiges
durch mich

Die Sonne
Umkreisend
Senket Göttlich=Geistiges
In mich

Die Erde
Von unten
Stützet Göttlich=Geistiges
In mir

Rudolf Steiner: Mantra
© *Ita Wegman Archiv, Arlesheim*

The Sufferings of the Nathan Soul

*Anthroposophic Christology
on the Eve of World War I*

Peter Selg

STEINERBOOKS
AN IMPRINT OF ANTHROPOSOPHIC PRESS, INC.
610 Main St., Great Barrington, MA 01230
www.steinerbooks.org

Copyright © 2016 by Peter Selg. All rights reserved. No part of this publication may be reproduced, stored in a retrieval system, or transmitted, in any form or by any means, electronic, mechanical, photocopying, recording, or otherwise, without the prior written permission of the publisher. This book was originally published in German as *Die Leiden der nathanischen Seele: Anthroposophische Christologie am Vorabend des Ersten Weltkriegs* (Verlag des Ita Wegman Instituts, Arlesheim, Switzerland, 2014).

Translated by Matthew Barton

Book design by William Jens Jensen

LIBRARY OF CONGRESS CONTROL NUMBER: 2015957150
ISBN: 978-1-62148-150-8 (paperback)
ISBN: 978-1-62148-151-5 (ebook)

Contents

Foreword ix

1. Rudolf Steiner: "The Four Christ Sacrifices 1
and the Culture of Selflessness" (Basel, June 1, 1914)

2. Preludes to the Mystery of Golgotha: 27
The account given in Basel, and the culmination of
anthroposophic Christology before
the outbreak of World War I

Notes and References 81

For Sergei

Christ did not come into the world and pass through the Mystery of Golgotha simply so that he might serve each one of us in our egoism. It would be terrible to think that people could comprehend the Pauline phrase "Not I but Christ in me" in terms of the Christ sustaining only a higher egoism in us. Christ died for the whole of humanity, for all humanity on earth! The Christ became earth's central and intrinsic spirit, with the task of redeeming for the earth all earthly spirit that flows out from human beings.
—**Rudolf Steiner** (July 16, 1914)

Foreword

It is certainly necessary to speak of such things, and this is because our friends need to stand up authentically for our cause and concerns, with a real inner love of truth and inner sense of truth—and with this alone. And by discussing this together, various things can become clearer in our minds.[1]

On June 1, 1914, Rudolf Steiner spoke in Basel for the last time before the outbreak of World War I, and for the last time ever in all his lectures and writings about the Nathan soul and its relationship with the Mystery of Golgotha. This internal lecture, given only for members of the Anthroposophical Society, concluded a series of profound Christological reflections begun on September 20, 1913, at the laying of the foundation stone for the St. John's building in nearby Dornach and culminating—four weeks before the assassination at Sarajevo—in the motif of "selflessness," whose importance for the future Rudolf Steiner stressed with great and, indeed, unmistakable emphasis.[2]

Basel had been a spiritual center of Steiner's activities since September 1905, when Steiner gave a lecture there entitled "The Overcoming of Materialism." A year after this first lecture, on September 20, 1906, exactly seven years before the foundation stone of the St. John's building was laid, the Paracelsus branch was also founded there. Besides 71 public and 42 members' lectures,[3] Steiner gave extensive lecture *cycles* in Basel in 1907, 1909, and 1912, on the Gospels of John, Luke, and Mark. In September 1909, during his lectures on the Gospel of St. Luke, Steiner for the first time focused closely on the being of Nathan. In Basel, too, the laying of the foundation stone in Dornach was picked up with a special echo and resonance. Just two days after this ceremonial event in Dornach, Rudolf Steiner stayed at the guesthouse of the Paracelsus branch at Ruemlinbachweg 10, and there—during the first annual general meeting of the Dornach St. John's Building Association—looked back upon this festive moment.

As in Dornach at the laying of the foundation stone, Rudolf Steiner also spoke in Basel of the "cry currently reverberating through humanity like a question from agonized and fearful humanity."[4] He described this foundation stone as a symbolic answer to the "cry of the human soul that fearfully avoids knowledge."[5] The foundation stone, he said, should signify "love, insight, and powerful strength" but would at the same time become a stumbling block and an irritation to many. Anthroposophic work, he went on, was only encountering the first of its problems at present, but would nevertheless remain uncompromising in continuing "to do what it must to serve and realize the truth."[6] He spoke of a "deceitful culture of the modern era," and in Basel pointed to the profoundly serious and urgent needs of the times. There, too, he presented the harrowing "macrocosmic Lord's Prayer" ("the evils hold sway...") from the "Fifth Gospel," which had first resounded two days previously at the building site in Dornach. ("Whereas inner bliss arose from the Lord's Prayer in the fourth post-Atlantean era, the knowledge humanity needs from now on can flow to us from this Lord's Prayer, whose phrases are structured in a way that shows us why evils hold sway, and why the human being needs to rebuild his body anew."[7])

Eight and a half months later, when Rudolf Steiner gave his lecture on the Nathan soul and the Christ sacrifice in the Basel branch, on June 1, 1914, the cupolas of the Dornach building were already in place, and soon afterward were roofed in tiles of Norwegian slate. Before this, in April, soon after the passing of Christian Morgenstern and his cremation in Basel, Rudolf Steiner had announced that the construction work on the building would take longer than envisaged, and the opening celebrations would therefore not take place in August. Despite this, in the months before war broke out, work on the building continued unabated, with support and advice from Steiner, whose lectures in various cities during this time turned with great intensity to Christological themes, encompassing the current spiritual situation of the times, the building project in Dornach, and the planned "School of Spiritual Science."[8] His accounts of the "Fifth Gospel" (from October 1, 1913) and of the "Preparatory Stages of the Mystery of Golgotha" (given from December 30, 1913, on) mark an unmistakable culmination of anthroposophic Christology.

In 1914 Steiner also spoke in public about certain aspects of this newly propounded awareness of Christ. In January 1914 in Berlin, for instance, he spoke of "Christ in the twentieth century," and in February in Hannover, on the theme "From Jesus to Christ." But it was *only* to members that he developed the spiritual core of his comments on the "Fifth Gospel" and the "Preparatory Stages of the Mystery of Golgotha," the latter centered on the connection between the Nathan soul and the Christ being. He did so in the hope that this content would be treated confidentially and deepened in meditative reflection.[9] We do not know how many members of the Anthroposophical Society actually undertook this in the months preceding World War I, nor whether these members were aware of the whole context of history and consciousness in which these moving accounts by Steiner doubtless stood. In his lectures on the "Fifth Gospel" in particular, he repeatedly indicated the active nature of the reception or participation he was hoping for from his audience; and also that these spiritual contents and the paths of schooling associated with them would be an absolute necessity in the future. Looking back now—as we can—it becomes clear that Steiner not only offered deep insights into the sufferings intrinsic to modern times and the near future, but also sought to prepare people for dire forthcoming events, and nurture in them some form of inner, spiritual resistance.

To mark the hundredth anniversary of the first outbreak of war in 1914, we here reprint the Basel lecture of June 1, 1914, which was previously published as a single lecture in 1936 and 1949 under the title of "The Four Christ Sacrifices. The Three Preparatory Stages of the Mystery of Golgotha." The identical text was incorporated into *The Collected Works of Rudolf Steiner* (CW) as volume 152 in 1964 (as "Preparatory Stages to the Mystery of Golgotha"). The lecture was originally taken down in shorthand by Rudolf Hahn, a member of the Basel branch, and of the St. John's Building Association in Dornach. However, the vitally important introductory words that Steiner spoke on June 1, 1914, in Basel were not included in CW 152, but were planned for inclusion in a later compilation on the history of the anthroposophic movement and the Anthroposophical Society. Hitherto they were only published in 1936 in Newsletter no.

39, "What is Happening in the Anthroposophical Society," of the weekly periodical *Das Goetheanum* (September 27, 1936, pp. 153–155). Below, these words are reunited with the text of the lecture. The second part of this book offers a study of Rudolf Steiner's over-arching intentions in his lectures on "Preparatory Stages of the Mystery of Golgotha," closely connected as these are with the "Fifth Gospel." It is not by chance that they were given on the eve of that great global catastrophe that engulfed Europe and the world in disaster, and that still continues to reverberate. In an "age of extremes" however, as Eric Hobsbawm calls our era, these accounts by Rudolf Steiner, or the soul-spiritual developmental potentials he reveals in them—which are relevant also to the anthroposophic movement itself—likewise continue to be alive and resonant.

My warm thanks to members of the Paracelsus Branch in Basel—to whom I spoke in the spring of this year about Rudolf Steiner's lecture of June 1, 1914—for indirectly making this book possible.

Peter Selg
Ita Wegman Institute
Arlesheim, June 2014

Rudolf Steiner

*The Four Christ Sacrifices
and the Culture of Selflessness*

Basel, June 1, 1914

Rudolf Steiner: the countenance of Christ. Wooden sculpture of the "Representative of Humanity" (Goetheanum, Dornach)

At the time when railways were slowly being introduced in Europe, a question arose on one occasion as to whether a railway line should or should not be laid from Potsdam to Berlin. At the time, Berlin's Postmaster General said this: "I cannot imagine this to be necessary. Every week I give the order for so and so many stagecoaches to leave Berlin for Potsdam, and no one ever rides in them. Why therefore do we need trains between Berlin and Potsdam?" Nevertheless, a line was established, and though the stagecoaches had been empty, a great many people were soon traveling this route by train.

When the Austrian physician Kisch was still a young man, he once traveled to a medical conference. In the train on the way he met the renowned medical professor Virchov. If Kisch had been older the nature of their conversation would probably have been different. However, being young, he spoke to Virchov about the possibility of knowing something about the workings of providence, about the existence of a divine, cosmic being, a wise governance of the universe. Now, Virchov was not only a great scholar, but also a well-meaning man, and he listened to this young badger (forgive me the expression) and then said to him, "My dear young colleague, I advise you not to spend any further time with things the human brain is not constructed for." Thus you see that the Postmaster General thought it unnecessary to build a railway line from Berlin to Potsdam, and yet the railway was built; and the great pathologist Virchov did not believe that the human brain was constructed for suprasensory knowledge, but nevertheless, suprasensory knowledge will find entry into the spiritual culture of humankind!

A little while back, not far from this place, someone stated that this "Anthroposophy," this spiritual-scientific worldview, concerned all kinds of merely fantastical things that could amount to no more than elaborate hypotheses. It was pointed out to the person in question that at the time Copernicus, say, or Giordano Bruno or Galileo were propounding the modern worldview of astronomy, people also regarded this as a system of elaborate fantasy. He retorted that the Copernican worldview, the sun's rotation around the earth, is something different from recurring lives on earth. This rotation, he said, was a fact, whereas recurring lives on earth were not. This gentleman—or his like—have taken about 400 years to arrive at the view that the Copernican system is a fact or reality. At the time they, or their kind, did not recognize that they were being presented with facts; they only acknowledged this retrospectively. A time will come when recurring lives and other facts of spiritual science will also be recognized by such people as reality.

Yet the force of this man's reply betrayed his lack of awareness of the real foundations of the Copernican system. He is one of those who fail to acknowledge the diverse intermediate conclusions from which the Copernican system emerged. He pictures the "fact" of this system really as if those who propounded it could have taken one or several chairs and placed them out in the cosmos, looking back from this position to see the sun in the middle and the planets revolving around it.

This is the kind of picture conveyed to children in school, and it entirely obscures reality, and the actual foundations of our Copernican system.

A huge arrogance is prevalent in all scientific thinking nowadays. As soon as we take a closer look at the real nature of this thinking, we inevitably encounter some very problematic things. Our contemporaries, especially those who most pride themselves on their scientific logic, practice a logic that is actually very, very flawed and short-sighted. Sometimes it is important to take a good, hard look at such things, so as to give a little less credence, at least in our own circles, to the value of the objections repeatedly raised against spiritual science. It is so easy to be drawn into questioning what this or that "authority" thinks of spiritual science, and to give his opinion a good deal of weight. Before hearkening so easily to an authority of this kind, it is a good idea to engage a little more with the nature of the logic, in particular its scope, the scope of thinking, of figures who are highly regarded today. We will always encounter those who say that what spiritual science presents is only an article of faith; it requires belief in its assertions. Our powers of understanding cannot actually approach and engage with this spiritual science. As far as ordinary philosophy is concerned—at least where people today regard it as healthy and of a more materialistic hue—or in relation to some other field of study, people think they can approach and engage with it with their ordinary understanding, whereas the results of spiritual-scientific enquiry require only their faith.

But someone who truly seeks to stand upon a spiritual-scientific foundation must counter this by reminding people, continually, that very fundamental requirements are not being met across broad swathes of modern life; fundamental requirements intrinsic to gaining real understanding of what the science of the spirit has to offer the culture of today and tomorrow. In fact, by far the majority of people today will regard it only as paradoxical, grotesque, when we speak of these fundamental requirements necessary for understanding spiritual science.

I would like to tell you about an experience I had in the last few days—not in order to speak personally, but simply to illustrate the lack of insight today into the fundamental conditions really needed to grasp scientific truths. The personal aspect is of no account here. I was giving some lectures in Paris, including one to a carefully chosen audience ("Clairvoyance, Reason and Science" on May 26, 1914). A few days later an article appeared in a French periodical. It is assumed, though it would be better if it wasn't, that an outsider who attends such a talk and then writes about it, has the wherewithal to judge what he has heard. People can only imagine that this is the point of him writing the article. It would seem grotesque for most modern minds to imagine that someone with no capacity for judging it should write such an article. But this is what we find when we examine the fundamental requirements for understanding spiritual science, as we must. This article contains something that seemingly has nothing to do with the lecture I gave. It figures already in paragraph three, where the author states, "Dr. Steiner was born in Bohemia, but culturally speaking he is very much a Hungarian." Well, it isn't true that I was born in Bohemia. I wouldn't object to being born there; it would be a fine thing to be born there. It just happens to be untrue. I will leave the author's second statement to your own judgement. Now aside from anything personal here, we have to be clear that someone who writes such twaddle does not meet even the lowest standards of truth. If he writes such palpable nonsense, it is clear that he is a stranger to the truth, has no sense of truth. Now in seeking to understand realities of the world of spirit, it is important—whether you believe me or not—to have a sense of truth that obliges us, whenever we say or write something, to study things truly and carefully and to write only what we know.

Thus, one of the fundamental requirements for spiritual science—and a feeling for this needs to become widespread—is to write and say only what we positively know to be true. Just imagine, if a miraculous epidemic spread across the globe tomorrow morning, which meant that people only wrote what they actually know, it is likely that most newspapers would no longer appear. In epidemic proportions, with people saying only what they actually know, most auditoriums might be left empty in consequence. Here then we have a fundamental requirement that is never met; and inevitably, if people have so little sense of the truth that they write the nonsense I quoted, then everything else they write about the event is worthless, too. They have failed to meet the fundamental requirement intrinsic to writing—not to say what one thinks is true, but to cultivate a real sense of truth and to follow where it leads.

There are many other fundamental requirements not met today. A small portion of self-knowledge is not enough to understand spiritual science. But even this little portion of self-knowledge is sometimes lacking where people judge things with unbelievable arrogance. I don't wish to speak—really I don't—of current situations; but what is happening at present does draw our attention to some deeper symptoms of the times. I felt obliged to dispute the overbearing opinion of a theologian about our science of the spirit, and felt it necessary to say that there was something unchristian in this attitude—a harsh rebuke for a theologian. But one has to call to mind the whole context that produced the little pamphlet "What is spiritual science about?" or at least the essay on which this was based. Just a few days back the author found fault with this expression—unchristian—saying it was impermissible to say such a thing, that one shouldn't resort to such derogatory phrases. Yet, if the person concerned had had just the tiniest amount of self-knowledge he, for his part, would have avoided another phrase that amounts to about the same. He said that spiritual science was a "crazy hotchpotch" and described the building in Dornach as a "gasworks." Well, we can argue about the meaning of "Christian"; is it disparaging the building in Dornach as a "gasworks" or seriously suggesting that something is "unchristian"?

We do not have to engage with every opinion, since here a single note is the whole of the music. We do not have to engage with all opinions since actually an exchange in which phrases such as "crazy hotchpotch" and "gasworks" are used is terribly comical. Nowadays much is said about a sense of truth and tolerance. In the pamphlet I spoke of, you can find this sentence: "We wish to practice tolerance toward views that accord with the Swiss constitution..."; truly, unbelievably comical! If you imagine translating this sentence into Turkish, it would read, "We wish to practice a tolerance that accords with Turkish views"...and so forth. Well, sometimes it is good to draw attention to such things. Sometimes, rather than just scrutinizing things in a cold and logical way, they refute themselves by our efforts not to laugh out loud!

We have to highlight such things, because our friends do need to take an authentic stance; they must stand up for our cause with a real inner love of truth and sense of truth. Various things become clearer when we discuss them together. It is all too understandable that we overlook or ignore the kinds of texts that have just been referred to. But an occultist cannot do so since he also senses in them something intimately connected with the author's character of soul. I am not saying all this simply in order to castigate the modern world in general or the kinds of things surrounding us, but because these offer immediate examples of what our time lacks—what is really lacking—and inhibits understanding of spiritual-scientific truths that are so necessary for the true advancement of culture.

What our time needs above all is a new knowledge and perception of Christ increasingly gained by allowing the findings of spiritual science to inform us. And it is precisely Christian officialdom that often opposes such knowledge of Christ in our day. What we need for our culture is to develop a school of selflessness, and this insight must increasingly arise. A renewal of morality, a deepening of human ethical life, can only come about if we school ourselves in selflessness. This schooling of selflessness is something we can only undergo in the conditions that obtain in our current evolutionary era if we also understand what selflessness really is—gain a thorough understanding of the real nature of selflessness. If we reflect on the evolution of the cosmos, we can find no profounder example of selflessness than that given us in the appearance of Christ on earth. And to perceive the Christ means to pass through the school of selflessness. To perceive Christ means to acquaint ourselves with all the impulses in humanity's evolution that filter into our soul in a way that glows and warms through everything in this soul that has the capacity for selflessness, eliciting our active soulfulness and selflessness. Under the influence of materialism, humanity's capacity for selflessness has been lost, although this will only be recognized in future times. But by a deepening preoccupation with the Mystery of Golgotha, by penetrating knowledge of the Mystery of Golgotha with our whole feeling, our whole inner being, we can begin to reacquire a culture of selflessness.

And we can say that what Christ accomplished for earthly evolution is implicit in the basic impulse of selflessness, and that this impulse can engender a schooling of selflessness for conscious development of the human soul! We can best recognize this when we consider the whole, great context of the Mystery of Golgotha.

As we know it, this Mystery of Golgotha unfolded once only within physical earth evolution. On a single occasion, the being we acknowledge as Christ assumed corporeal existence in a human body, that of Jesus of Nazareth. But this Mystery of Golgotha has three preliminary stages. It was preceded by a threefold occurrence, albeit not on earth but in the world of spirit. In a sense, then, we have three Mysteries of Golgotha that did not as yet occur on the physical plane. Only the fourth took place on the physical plane, as the event of which the Gospels and Paul's Epistles tell us. Three supraterrestrial events occurred in preparation for this greatest of all earthly events. One of these supraterrestrial occurrences fell in the time of ancient Lemuria, and the other two during the Atlantean era. The fourth in this sequence, the Mystery of Golgotha itself, occurred in the post-Atlantean period.

The three preceding occurrences did not happen on earth but in the supraearthly world, and yet their power penetrated to the earth. Let us now try to comprehend how the powers of these three preparatory, supraearthly events preceding the Mystery of Golgotha worked into the evolution of humanity.

We have not yet become selfless in terms of our morality, our understanding of the world, and what unfolds within our consciousness soul; this is a mission we need to embrace in contemporary culture as it moves toward the future. Humanity must become ever more selfless, and it is this that will inform the future of truly ethical actions, the future of all loving deeds that earthly humanity can accomplish. Our conscious life is embarking on a selfless path, or rather it must embark upon it. But in a certain respect, something essentially selfless does already exist in us. It would be the greatest misfortune for earthly human beings if they were as self-seeking in certain aspects of their being as they still inevitably are in their moral, intellectual, and emotional life. If we became egoistic in our sense perceptions to the same degree that this is true of our morality, this would be the greatest possible misfortune for us. You see, the action of our bodily senses is really an expression of selflessness.

We possess bodily eyes and we see by means of them. However, we see only because the eyes are in fact selfless and we therefore have no sense of them at all. We carry them within us, as it were, seeing things through them, but the eyes themselves are extinguished in our perceptions. The same is true, too, of the other senses. We perceive the world by virtue of the fact that our senses are selfless. Let us assume for a moment that our eyes were selfish. What would happen to us? As we approached the color blue, for instance, instead of allowing the color through, this blue would be expended within the eye itself. Our eye would be sucked empty by it in a sense. If the eye could become as selfish as we are in our moral, intellectual, and feeling life, we would experience a kind of force of suction in the eye in response to blue. If when we approached the color red, our eye did not behave in a selfless way but sought to experience the full effect of red within itself, this effect would be something like stinging. Our selfish eye would respond to all visual impressions with a pain of either suction or stinging. We would be aware of having eyes, but we would perceive only sucking or stinging pain in them. In fact, as we go through the world, we become aware of color and light effects without having to think about our eyes, which extinguish themselves selflessly as we see. And this is true, too, of our other senses.

Selflessness holds sway in our senses; and yet they would not have arrived at this state, and would have been deprived of this selflessness already in the Lemurian era, if Lucifer had been at liberty to pursue his ends unhindered at that time. The spirit of which the Bible rightly says that "Your eye shall be opened..." necessitated that the human being was placed into a sphere of earthly life in which his eyes would have become selfish if they had evolved as they inevitably would under Lucifer's influence. Every sense impression—not only visual ones—would then have plagued humankind with something like a stinging in the eye instead of the perception of red, or a suction in the eye instead of the perception of blue. This danger was averted back in Lemurian times, and human evolution was protected from it, by the being who later assumed corporeal incarnation in the body of Jesus of Nazareth and passed through the Mystery of Golgotha. Not on the earth but in supraearthly worlds, this being ensouled itself—I cannot say incarnated—in an archangel being, a being from the hierarchy of the archangeloi. Thus while the earth was passing through the Lemurian period, in spiritual heights, in a kind of prefiguring of the John baptism, an archangel sacrificed his soul being to allow the Christ to imbue it; and by this means he released a power that worked into human evolution on earth. This influence resulted in a calming of the senses, their harmonious development. We can use our senses today because they are selfless; and when we have understood this and can show due gratitude for it to the world order, we will look back to ancient times and recognize that we owe to the first Christ sacrifice our sensory nature, which enables us to feel and perceive the glories of the natural world rather than sense-engendered pain. By ensouling himself in an archangel, Christ diverted from human evolution the danger of self-seeking senses; and this was the first preliminary stage of the Mystery of Golgotha.

The human being will gradually learn to develop a profound and important religious sense when he gazes upon the glories of the natural world, when he looks up to the starry heavens and upon everything sun-illumined in the animal, plant, and mineral kingdoms around us. He will learn to say this: I owe to the first sacrifice of Christ, which was a prelude and preparation for the Mystery of Golgotha, the fact that I can see the world around me, that I stand amidst this world, and my senses are not a source of pain but an instrument through which I can perceive the beauty of the world. If we look ahead into the future, we can see a time when the enjoyment of nature will be Christ-permeated. Then, when people go out into nature and rejoice in the glories of spring, in the beauties of summer or other natural wonders, they will feel, and will say, that their delight in absorbing impressions of natural beauty around them must include an awareness that it is not them but Christ in their senses who endows them with the capacity to sense and perceive the glories of nature.

Now in the first periods of Atlantean evolution, due to the influence of Lucifer and Ahriman, another system of the human organism, that of our major organs, was at risk of falling prey to selfishness. If we reflect on the essential nature of our living organism we need only think how things would go for us if the function of these organs were impaired, as happens when they are affected by organic disorders. Here we can begin to experience a kind of selfishness in our lungs, heart, stomach, or other organs. Feeling pain in any one of these, we suddenly know that we have a stomach or heart and so forth. We have immediate awareness of these organs, and to suffer from such a disorder means that one of them has become selfish and is leading its own separate existence within our organism. In ordinary human life this is not the case. Our various organs live together in our whole organism in a selfless way, and our normal state is one where this fact allows us to maintain our coherence in the world, to live our lives with selfless organs and not to feel that we possess a stomach, lungs, and so on. Instead we have these organs without feeling them. They do not assert their individual existence but serve the whole organism.

On another occasion we will speak of why illness is induced by organs becoming selfish. Today let us only consider our normal state. If all had depended on Ahriman and Lucifer, very different conditions would have developed during Atlantean evolution; every single human organ would have become self-seeking, selfish, and something very curious would have happened. Assume someone approached a fruit, in other words something living in the outer world that we can eat or enjoy, or that has some relationship or other to our bodily organism. This very relationship will at some point in the future become a subject of medical study, once scientists allow spiritual science to stimulate and inspire them. At this point people will realize that when someone picks cherries, say, from a tree and eats them, what enters the organism with these cherries has a particular connection with certain organs, while other kinds of fruit have other relationships with other organs. Everything that we introduce into the human organism has certain relationships and connections with this organism.

If what Ahriman and Lucifer instigated in the Atlantean period had come to full effect then, when we picked cherries for instance, the organ connected with cherries would have formed the greatest greed and desire for them. An infinite desire would have come to expression, and the human being would have felt this particular organ selfishly detaching itself from the whole organism. The other organs likewise would have been in conflict with each other within the human organism. Or let us take another example; imagine something is present that can harm a person, for just as things in nature have good, beneficial relationships with us, so others have destructive or detrimental ones. If a person were then to approach a poisonous plant or something similar with only negative connections with a particular organ, one would sense this connection through the organ's inner activity, and this would express itself in a terrible, tormenting feeling of anxiety. One would feel confronted by something whose influence on that organ is to make it feel cauterized.

But now let us consider not the human being but the surrounding air. Everything the air contains has a relationship with our organs. If what Ahriman and Lucifer desired had been fulfilled, if the human being had been completely self-dependent, one would have been driven through the world either by the most bestial desire for what is agreeable to one or another organ, or by terrible repulsion from what can harm them. Imagine us placed in the world with bodily organs that made us, at most, a plaything of every pleasant smell that we would run after even if the source of it were an hour away; or made to flee by feelings of repulsion emanating from faraway. If we were thrown back and forth like this, like a rubber ball, how could we possibly evolve in the world? But instead of this our primary organs were dulled in this respect, were harmonized; and this is because, during the first Atlantean period of evolution, the second preliminary stage of the Mystery of Golgotha occurred in supraearthly spheres.

Once again the Christ being ensouled himself in an archangel being, and what this brought about shone down into the earth's atmosphere. This caused the major organs to be assuaged and harmonized, and rendered them selfless within us. In our co-existence with the outer world we would continually be exposed to the worst illnesses and could never be healthy if this second Christ event had not occurred. And again, as a future perspective, when humanity imbues itself with real understanding of the world of spirit, it will acquire a sense of gratitude toward the spirit beings upon whom we are dependent. Then humanity will fill itself with a true piety that will lead people to express their sense that they can only be a physical human being with selfless organs because they did not evolve unaided in the world. Christ in me, they will say, has shaped my organs so that I can be a human being. Increasingly, therefore, we learn that everything that makes us human must be understood in terms of "Not I but Christ in me." Christ has safeguarded the whole of humanity's evolution in the three preludes to the Mystery of Golgotha, which he accomplished before this Mystery itself.

At the latter end of Atlantean evolution, humanity faced a third danger, in which thinking, feeling, and will were at risk of falling into disorder. Selfishness would have found its way into our human thinking, feeling, and will. What would this have led to? Well, a person would have wished or willed something, would have pursued these will impulses, while his thinking pursued a different impulse, and his feeling yet another. It was necessary for human evolution that thinking, feeling, and will were integrated within the soul's totality as selfless faculties. They could not have been, under the influence of Lucifer and Ahriman alone, and so thinking, feeling, and will would have become egoistic, as it were destroying the soul's harmonious action.

Thus, the third Christ event occurred toward the end of the Atlantean period, and once again the Christ being ensouled himself in an archangel, and the power arising in the supraearthly world by virtue of this made possible a harmonization of thinking, feeling, and will. Truly, just as physical sunrays must work down upon the earth so that all plant life can burgeon, so the sun spirit must be reflected down from supraearthly worlds to the earth as I have described. At this third stage he harmonized thinking, feeling, and will as these needed to be harmonized in ordinary human life.

What would have become of the human being if this third Christ event had not occurred? He would have been driven like the furies by his wild passions, by his will life. Frenzied on the one hand, on the other his rational mind could have looked down scornfully on what his raging will was doing. This was averted by the third Christ event, when, for the third time the Christ lived in the outward soul of an archangel, a being from the hierarchy of the archangeloi.

Humanity has retained a memory of how human passions and human thinking were harmonized by the powers that at that time worked down from supraearthly worlds. Although misunderstood, this memory symbol is preserved in the figure of St. George who conquers the dragon, or Michael who conquers the dragon, symbolizing the third Christ event when Christ ensouled himself in archangel form. And the dragon he treads underfoot is the one who has brought human thinking, feeling, and will into disorder. All who look upon St. George with the dragon or Michael with the dragon, or similar images are in truth speaking of the third Christ event. Moreover, the Greeks who, in their wonderful mythology, created something like after-images of what happened in the world of spirit at the end of the Atlantean period, revered the sun spirit as the harmonizer of thinking, feeling, and will in the human being. The ancient Greeks who knew something of these things spoke thus: You sun spirit, you have ensouled yourself in etheric spirit form (for that is the form of those whom we nowadays call archangels). Upon your wondrous lyre you have reconciled the thinking, feeling, and will that would otherwise run wild and untamed in the human soul. Upon this lyre resound the harmonious tones of the human soul.

Thus the sun spirit became the guardian and protector of the frenzied passions raging in the human being when, as happened, these surfaced in the wild vapours that rise from the interior of the earth, break through its surface. If we were exposed to these vapors and allowed them to influence us, our thinking, feeling, and will would rage through one another in wild tumult and disorder. Thus, the ancient Greeks set the Pythia over these earth-rising vapors that, instigated by Lucifer and Ahriman, sowed disorder and confusion in human passions. Apollo conquered these wild passions; he was the overlighting spirit of the Pythia, who became an oracle and prophet. In the sun spirit Apollo, the Greeks experienced the Christ of the third Christ event; and in the mood of the Pythia who ruled human passions, in this power of protection with which the god Apollo endowed the Pythia, they saw the influence of the third Christ sacrifice—the harmonizing of the chaos of human passions by the third Christ event. The sun spirit Apollo, however, was for the Greeks basically the same power as is depicted in the image of Michael or St. George conquering the dragon.

Therefore, we can see the meaning of a curious saying by the martyr Justin, which we must also regard as Christian even if various modern representatives of Christianity would think it heretical. Justin said that Heraclitus, Socrates, and Plato were Christians, although only in the way one could be a Christian before the Mystery of Golgotha. Modern theologians no longer understand such a thing, yet the Christian martyrs of the early Christian era were aware that the ancient Greeks, even if they did not use the name of Christ, drew on mystery knowledge and knew that Apollo embodies the great sun spirit who will later indwell a human being. In Apollo the ancient Greeks saw this sun being ensouled in the figure of an archangel.

Then came the fourth, earthly mystery, that of Golgotha. The same Christ being who ensouled himself three times in the form of an archangel now took corporeal form in the body of Jesus of Nazareth at the event we know as the baptism in Jordan.

I acknowledge that you will think it strange if I say that this being ensouled himself three times in the form of an archangel and then in human form, for it would seem more rational, and more schematic if, between ensoulment in archangel form and in human form there was an ensoulment in angelic form—that is, if the Christ had ensouled himself at one of these prior stages in the form of an angel. This is how it seems. But even if many object that spiritual-scientific matters are inventions, truly it is not so, and you will see this from other things as well. And if you ask me why Christ did not descend gradually from hierarchy to hierarchy, and thence took human form, I am obliged to say that I do not know since this is not a matter of rational judgment. My enquiries into the actual realities show that Christ employed an archangel form on three occasions and did not employ that of an angel; and then took on a human form. I must leave it to subsequent enquiries to ascertain why this is so. At present I do not yet know the reason for it. But it is so. As you can see from what I have said, if one were simply to invent these things one would do it very differently.

Thus the fourth stage of the Mystery of Golgotha occurred, and averted another danger in which, through the influence of Lucifer and Ahriman, the human "I" would have fallen into disarray. In the Lemurian period human sense organs would have fallen into disarray through Lucifer; in the early Atlantean period the human body's life organs would have succumbed to disorder and disharmony; and in the later Atlantean period the organs underlying thinking, feeling, and willing would have succumbed. In the post-Atlantean era the "I" itself was at risk of disorder and confusion. Since at this time the "I" needed to find its place in human evolution, efforts were made to establish harmony between this "I" and the powers of the cosmos so that the "I" would not become a plaything tossed hither and thither between them. This is what could have happened. The "I" could have failed to develop the capacity to retain its entity as self. If it had been delivered up to these powers of the cosmos, what comes from the soul would have been torn away by all elemental forces originating in wind, air, and waves. The human being would have been borne away everywhere by these forces.

Michelangelo painted this. Take a look at his works; he painted what was threatening the human being, what emerges in the sibyls. In a wonderful way he depicted the human who feels his "I" falling into disarray; as it does so, all kinds of wonderful wisdom can emerge but without the person being able to control or direct it. Take a look at these pictures by Michelangelo; they depict the diverse stages of what is given up to the elemental beings through the disarray of the "I." Other things are depicted, too, though. In the same room he painted the pondering figures of prophecy who, as one can see, shine with the quality that preserves order in the "I" in relation to the cosmos. It is wonderfully moving to see this striving for the "I" in the figures of the prophets, and on the other hand the human figures who have fallen into disarray through the "I" itself; and then in this same room, in human, corporeal form, the Christ himself whose mission it is to create order in the "I" that must enter the world.

Yes, spiritual science will continually deepen our insight into how this human "I" can attain selflessness through the fourth Christ event, the Mystery of Golgotha. Our senses have said, Not I but Christ in us. Our life organs have said, Not I but Christ in us. The organs of sensibility have said, Not I but Christ in us. Moreover, the human being's moral and intellectual life must also learn to say, Not I but Christ in me. We see this at every step we take into the world of spirit.

This is what I wished to discuss today so that on a future occasion, hopefully very soon, we will be able to offer occult evidence of these realities and show that what we call spiritual science can flow into our moral and intellectual life to enable people to become pupils of selflessness in whom the Christ lives. Then we can feel the Christ alive in us in every word spoken about the science of the spirit.

But there is one further thing I wish to say. As you know, since 1909 we have been performing our mystery plays in Munich. These productions may be regarded as good or bad—that is not the important thing here. But what has been accomplished there required a certain energy, a strength we do not have simply by being human on earth. You see, in Dornach, when we undertake sculptural work on various kinds of hardwood, we need muscle power. We cannot say that we can consciously give ourselves this muscle power; it comes from our body, and our inner capacities. It is not something we can dictate. Nor can we dictate or determine what we accomplish spiritually, for which we need spiritual strength. This is not solely dependent on our inherent gifts as a human being, just as it does not depend on these alone whether we can do something physically. It depends also on our body's muscular strength. Thus we need spiritual powers that are just as much external to us as our muscular strength is external to our soul. I know that superficially it might seem idiotic to think spiritual powers flow in from without, rather than rising up from within us. People are welcome to think me an idiot, but their cleverness reminds me of someone who cannot distinguish hunger from a slice of bread. Spiritual powers flow into us, and the bread comes to us from without. It would be crazy to imagine that our hunger itself creates the bread that satisfies it. In the same way, the power of *our* soul does not engender the powers we need for spiritual activity. These must flow into us, flow to us. And just as we very well know, if we are not crazy, that our hunger is in us and the bread comes to us from without, so those who live in worlds of spirit know what is within them and what comes from without. Personally, since 1909, when I sought to develop what was needed for the mystery plays in all stillness and composure, I felt the spiritual power that came to me from without. I was aware that the spiritual eye of a spiritual being was resting upon what has been undertaken. I am describing my direct experience.

In the early period of our spiritual-scientific movement, when we were working in Germany, an individual approached us warmly and, with a wonderful enthusiasm, absorbed what we were able to offer at the time. Not only did he devotedly and enthusiastically take up everything that it was possible to present at the time in relation to humanity's evolution, cosmic secrets, reincarnation, and karma, but at the same time he brought a wonderful aesthetic sensibility to bear on all this. Everything that arose through teaching and discussion with this individual was imbued with beauty. Unlike nowadays, there were not very many of us at this time, and the room was by no means full when we gathered. The things we present today to a large audience were at that time discussed among only three—between two others and me. One of these two departed from the physical plane in 1904 already, entered the world of spirit. Naturally a process of development occurs after death, and in 1907, when we performed Schuré's reconstruction of the Mystery of Eleusis, no influence from her was as yet discernible. It began in 1909, and has continually increased over recent years. I was fully aware that this was the individuality of the person who had approached us so warmly, whose distinctive qualities elicited a truly objective love. From the spiritual world this spirit acted like a guardian angel for our efforts in marrying the aesthetic and the esoteric in our mysteries. One had the sense that this individuality who had withdrawn to the world of spirit back in 1904 was now protecting and safeguarding what has flowed into earthly reality and permeated us. Looking up gratefully to her we can experience how the eye of a spirit's soul has rested its gaze upon our actions.

But when it was a matter of engaging in conversations and dialogue with this individuality—well, we can call it dialogue because it is a kind of interaction—then this individual made clear that she could find a better point of contact with our work on earth the more we imbued ourselves with the thought of Christ within earthly evolution. If I were to clothe in earthly words what this individuality repeatedly expressed, I would say—and of course I can only give symbolic expression here to realities that are different in the world of spirit: "I find such good contact with you because you, for your part, increasingly find ways to make your spiritual science an expression of the living Word of Christ himself."

This is what the Christ impulse will become for us; the living bridge between the life of the earth and life in supraearthly worlds. In three stages, Christ in the suprasensory worlds endowed human beings with the core nature we need if we are to live rightly. In three stages Christ rendered aspects of the human being selfless—the senses, life organs, and sensory organs. Now it is up to human beings themselves to become selfless in intellectual and moral ways, learning to comprehend what the phrase "Not I but Christ in me" means in terms of human intellect and morality.

The world will come to see that the spiritual science we propound is the Word of Christ. He said, "I am with you always, even unto the end of the world." The mission of spiritual science in our time is to open the doors to the living Christ. The dead unite with the living who understand that Christ found the transition from heavenly to earthly work. When the dead incline to those alive on earth as their closest protective guardians, they find the souls of those living on earth all the more intensively the more these souls themselves are pervaded and spiritualized by the Christ impulse. Christ descended as sublime sun spirit from supraearthly worlds through the Mystery of Golgotha so that he might find a dwelling in human souls. Spiritual science is to be the message of how Christ can dwell in our souls. When Christ finds his dwelling place in human souls on earth, the Christ strength will shine back from the earth's aura into the worlds from which the Christ departed to redeem earthly humankind, and then the whole cosmos will be Christ-filled.

We gradually raise ourselves to this profound understanding of the Mystery of Golgotha if we really imbue ourselves with spiritual science. If we reflect on this, reflect also that spiritual science must be a school of selflessness for humanity's future intellectual and moral life, and then we can realize all the more fully that spiritual science must proclaim the Mystery of Golgotha—and then we will know the meaning of the spiritual-scientific impulses that seek entry into modern life. The Christ impulse must penetrate humanity, and truly all people can acknowledge and accept it because the Christ did not appear to one nation only, but, as the sublime being of the sun, belongs to the whole earth and can enter all human souls of any and every nation and religion. May people in great numbers find their way to such understanding of the Christ impulse, and of the Mystery of Golgotha. Then, perhaps, what many who bear the outward stamp of Christianity regard as unchristian and heretical will be seen as the most Christian thing of all.

A merely rational understanding of the Mystery of Golgotha is not enough; let us try to comprehend this Mystery of Golgotha with our whole soul, and acknowledge that we will need the science of the spirit to do so. And then we will also recognize that we, our souls, are part of a spiritual stream that knows what is necessary for humanity both now and in the near future.

These were the things I wanted to speak to you about today. I hope that we will be able to continue reflections closely related to these, in this city, in the not too distant future.

2.

Preludes to the Mystery of Golgotha

*The account given in Basel,
and the culmination of anthroposophic
Christology before the outbreak of World War I.*

*Rudolf Steiner: Model for the Christ sculpture—
the Nathan Jesus child? (Goetheanum, Dornach)*

People will have to exchange the spirit of mere thought for that of immediate vision, for shared feeling and experience of the Christ who walks in living spirit beside all human souls.[10]

Rudolf Steiner began his lecture in Basel on June 1, 1914, in anecdotal and narrative mode. And yet from the outset he was considering very grave contemporary conditions and contexts, among other things the lack of capacity for truth and the "enormous pride and arrogance" of modern culture, along with its science—a civilization manifesting great, even "imperial" ambitions in all kinds of fields and disciplines, but with no stable ground beneath it.[11] In view of this situation, Rudolf Steiner warned his anthroposophic audience against revering too greatly "scientific authorities" or "scientific standards," instead urging them to develop their own capacity for judgement and self-awareness; and to find their way through to a certain degree of autonomy in their regard for Anthroposophy and their acknowledgement of its value. ("It is so easy to be drawn in to questioning what this or that 'authority' thinks of spiritual science, and to give one's opinion a good deal of weight. Before hearkening so easily to an authority of this kind, it is a good idea to engage a little more with the nature of the logic, in particular its scope, the scope of thinking, of figures who are highly regarded today.") In his introductory words he stressed the lack of the "fundamental requirements" in contemporary culture for real understanding of anthroposophic spiritual science—a fact that Steiner had again experienced shortly before this in Paris in the form of a farcical newspaper report on his public lecture of May 26 (to an audience of 400) that was just a further instance of many similar distortions.[12] As he would later do repeatedly in the subsequent war years, Rudolf Steiner here emphasized the lack of a "sense of truth" in newspaper reports (... "that obliges us, whenever we say or write something, to really study things carefully and to write only what we know"). Some newspaper reports had even made errors in regard to his biography, stating that he had been born in Bohemia. Six years previously, in 1908, the Jesuit priest Otto Zimmermann had written of Steiner's supposed Jewish descent;[13] and in the year before, 1913, another author (Karl Zoubek) had poured scorn and mockery on his book *Theosophy*, noting among other things:

> Rudolf Steiner is said to be from a Catholic family (and was born in Kraljevic in Hungary [*sic*]) and yet his thoughts approximate so closely to the Rabbinical inanities of the Talmud that, even if only through some unconscious inherited contamination, he is doubtless influenced by the latter. Like the hysterical Loyola, Steiner is likely to be a Semitic crossbreed. His speculative thoughts show a marked affinity with the founder of the Jesuit order. But we do not wish to see our nation rendered mentally unstable and perverse either by Roman or theosophical Jesuits.[14]

Like the assertions of Zimmermann or even the digressions of Zoubek, the newspaper report on Steiner's public lecture in Paris is really not worth mentioning. But the lies, distortion, and aggression it disseminated were certainly symptomatic of the time and of the dire approaching events about which Steiner had been speaking for some time. Week by week such reports also made it increasingly difficult for Anthroposophy and its building in Dornach to work effectively in the world. On September 20, 1913, the foundation stone of the new building had been laid in Dornah, and just five months later (on February 28, 1914) Rudolf Steiner had felt compelled to reply to an article by an Arlesheim priest, Riggenbach, in the *Birseck, Birsig and Leimental Daily News,* based on a lecture Riggenbach had given in the Reform Church in Arlesheim, entitled "What Do the Theosophists Want?" Steiner's response in the same paper was entitled "What is the Point of Spiritual Science?" Riggenbach had accused Steiner, among other things, of contradicting the Gospels in his theosophical and anthroposophical statements about the human suprasensory bodies, higher stages of knowledge, reincarnation and karma, and spiritual-scientific Christology. In his own article Steiner replied in a detailed, sober, and composed manner, saying for instance:

> It is quite wrong to accuse [Anthroposophy and Theosophy] of stating that Jesus did not mature into Christ from a young age, as shown in the Bible, under the guidance of the Holy Spirit but, in his first thirty years of life, only prepared his bodily sheath into which Christ descended at the Jordan baptism. What spiritual science has to say of these matters cannot be represented in a more distorted form than in this assertion. Spiritual science enquires into what actually happened at the Jordan baptism—this event that, without any doubt, appears in the Bible, too, as an event of great importance in the life of Jesus. (Weizsaecker even translates the important relevant passage in the Gospel of St. Luke, as "This is my beloved son; *this day have I engendered him.*") Spiritual-scientific enquiry finds that the spirit of Christ guided Jesus of Nazareth as if from without until his thirtieth birthday, then entered into his inmost being at that age.[15]

Anthroposophy, said Steiner in his reply to the Arlesheim priest, was endeavoring to "enlarge" and "heighten" the idea of Christ.[16] No doubt it was *this* exchange that, after Steiner's introductory words in Basel on June 1, 1914, formed part of the background to the real beginning of Steiner's lecture:

> What our time needs above all is a new knowledge and perception of Christ increasingly gained by allowing the findings of spiritual science to inform us. And it is precisely Christian officialdom that often opposes such knowledge of Christ in our day.

The key motif of the whole lecture—selflessness—as a decisive quality of the future, stood in polar opposition to what Steiner, in his introductory words, had described as "pride and arrogance" along with the lack of a "sense of truth":

> We have not yet become selfless in terms of our morality, our understanding of the world and what unfolds within our consciousness soul, and this is a mission we need to embrace in contemporary culture as it moves toward the future. Humanity must become ever more selfless, and it is this that will inform the future of truly ethical actions, the future of all loving deeds that earthly humanity can accomplish.

Clearer than ever before in any of his lectures and writings, and more clearly than at any later moment, Rudolf Steiner spoke in this lecture in Basel not just about a necessary quality of selflessness,[17] but of a *school of selflessness*. Only through this school or schooling was it possible, he said, to renew morality and deepen our ethical life, which would in turn be vital for the future of civilization. Such a school or schooling was predicated today on the awakening of real understanding for selflessness—and in the profoundest sense, he said, this understanding is possible through the appearance of the Christ being on earth.

At least in Rudolf Hahn's shorthand transcript of the lecture, which in many places clearly failed to record all the words Steiner spoke, these decisively important statements, key to the lecture's overall intentions, came one after another in a very close-knit, paratactic form, followed immediately by the thought that knowledge of Christ was the real foundation for acquiring selflessness: *"And to perceive the Christ means to pass through the school of selflessness."* The "school of selflessness" therefore at the same time means the "school of Christ." This was a matter of knowing and perceiving him, or of acquiring the "Christ consciousness," which Steiner first hinted at in Munich in 1909,[18] and, since the year before, 1913 (or since his lecture in London on May 2, 1913), was occupying a spiritually important and even decisive place in his teachings. In Basel he said:

> To perceive Christ means to acquaint ourselves with all the impulses in humanity's evolution that filter into our soul in a way that glows and warms through everything in this soul that has the capacity for selflessness, eliciting our active soulfulness and selflessness.

Here, albeit indirectly, it became apparent that gaining selflessness was a gradual process rather than a moral position or soul event enacted by a resolve and corresponding activation of will. Instead one should endeavor, through a Michaelic warmth process, to nurture the seeds of selflessness already present in the human soul life (an "already-selfless essence") in the "fire of being-creating love"—as Steiner was to formulate it years later when renewing Christian worship.¹⁹ After the end of World War I, which marked an initial culmination of the destructive forces of egoism, imperialism, and technology, along with the deaths of millions of victims, Steiner gave mantric form to these thoughts:

> Victorious spirit
> Flame through faint-hearted
> Tremulous souls,
> Burn up self-seeking,
> Kindle compassion
> So that selflessness—
> Humanity's life-stream—
> Hold sway as the source
> Of spirit's rebirth.²⁰

Selflessness can only be developed—as expression of the spiritual "flame," that is, of a will-governed moral warmth *process*—if we first "burn up self-seeking" and "kindle compassion."

As Rudolf Steiner emphasized in Basel on June 1, 1914, selflessness had almost been lost under the influence of materialism, and the tragic repercussions of this would only become apparent in future.²¹ Yet it was, he said, possible to reverse this—something that could (or must) occur through Christology, in other words through an *existential engagement* with the incarnation and life path of Christ Jesus. He regarded this as nothing to do with personal religious choice or preference, or with any academic debate in theology, but as a question that concerned humanity:

> But by a deepening preoccupation with the Mystery of Golgotha, by penetrating knowledge of the Mystery of

Golgotha with our whole feeling, our whole inner being, we can begin to reacquire a culture of selflessness.

This was, in Steiner's view, to do with a real participation in the so-called Mystery of Golgotha, by means of which it would be possible to achieve a transformation of civilization through a schooling path pursued by individuals, and through a new social orientation:

> And we can say that what Christ accomplished for earthly evolution is implicit in the basic impulse of selflessness, and that this impulse can engender a schooling of selflessness for conscious development of the human soul!

But to achieve this, and to follow the schooling path he outlines, with the aim of truly participating in the Mystery of Golgotha and fully comprehending it "with one's whole soul," Steiner believes that we need a full understanding of what actually occurred on the hill at Golgotha, and in the three years preceding it, from the Jordan baptism onward; everything that happened prior to this mystery, and everything that followed it. The Mystery of Golgotha should be considered in its "greater context," which is possible, he says, only with the help of anthroposophic spiritual science. With this in mind, we can understand what Steiner was suggesting in his reply to Father Riggenbach and then—among other things—examined more closely in the Basel lecture:

> What our time needs above all is a new knowledge and perception of Christ increasingly gained by allowing the findings of spiritual science to inform us. And it is precisely Christian officialdom that often opposes such knowledge of Christ in our day...

In Basel, as an integral part of the "greater context" of the Mystery of Golgotha, Rudolf Steiner described three "preludes" to it that occurred in the suprasensory world prior to the "greatest of all earthly events," and therefore both preceded and prepared for it. All three of these "preludes" and the Mystery of Golgotha itself, were clearly implicit in and determined by the key motif of selflessness (as the "fundamental impulse" of the Christ being), creating in the human being a *potential* "seed" of selflessness. This was to germinate and unfold in our subsequent evolution of consciousness in the battle with opposing powers and forces and in the passage through processes of sacrifice and warmth.

Continuing his account, Steiner described these "heavenly preludes" in detail, first describing an early evolutionary stage of the earth and humanity in "ancient Lemuria" (where our "intrinsic evolution really began"[22]). In Steiner's account, it was at this time that anti-Christian powers of Lucifer sought to impregnate the human senses, in order to embed "self-seeking" or egoism into this realm of the human organism, thus harnessing our sensory relation to the world to extreme forces of sympathy and antipathy—to "forces of suction" and "stinging pain" that would have plagued us with "torment." To obstruct such a development, or in other words to overcome Lucifer within the human being's sensory organism, Christ penetrated and "ensouled" himself in an archangel being. Steiner speaks of this as a first sacrifice by Christ, at the same time showing clearly that the archangel in question sacrificed himself (or his "soul being"). Thus a reciprocal (or shared) process of sacrifice occurred, and the power of this sacrifice ultimately shone down into earth evolution a quality that "assuaged" and "harmonized" the human senses. They could therefore (once again) become the selfless instruments of our perception of the world, and of its "glories." *"Selflessness holds sway in our senses."* This selflessness in our perception of nature was something that Steiner in this Basel lecture described not only as the foundation for "religious feeling" but a quality that could be further intensified in future. Without doubt the whole of Goetheanism is working in this direction and preparing its further development:

> If we look ahead into the future, we can see a time when the enjoyment of nature will be Christ-permeated. Then, when people go out into nature and rejoice in the glories of spring, in the beauties of summer or other natural wonders, they will feel, and will say, that their delight in absorbing impressions of natural beauty around them must include an awareness that it is not them but Christ in their senses who endows them with the capacity to sense and perceive the glories of nature.

On another occasion he put this succinctly as "Christ's light in our daylight..."[23]

Next Rudolf Steiner spoke about the early period of the Atlantean era when, after being vanquished in our peripheral sensory organization, luciferic powers—in common with the intensifying influences of Ahriman—sought to penetrate and govern the inner organs of the human body. The human being's life organs were no longer to selflessly serve the whole organism but to assert themselves separately—in other words, organically determining and dictating the relationship with our surroundings and making us playthings of organic impressions and reactions (ranging from "greed" to "repulsion"). This would have predisposed our bodily nature to disorder and illness. Once again, however, the Christ accomplished a sacrifice and for the second time "ensouled" himself in an archangel being. Once again, the consequences of this deed streamed into earth's atmosphere, "assuaging" and "harmonizing" the life organs. Through this deed Christ reconfigured these organs so that it would be possible for us to remain human in future and to evolve further. "Christ gives me my human nature."[24] "Not I but Christ in me."

Finally in his Basel lecture, Steiner described a third Christ sacrifice in the latter period of ancient Atlantean evolution, when the luciferic–ahrimanic powers of self-seeking or egoism entered the human being's soul organization and proceeded to fragment a previously harmonious unity of thinking, feeling, and will, thus undermining the foundations for true human "I"-development. Having been twice vanquished (at least to a very great degree) in their attacks on both peripheral sense organs and central life organs, and overcome through Christ's sacrifice, the adversary powers now attempted to encroach on the human soul. Once again they sought to establish an autonomy—an apparent emancipation—of separate organs (this time in the soul realm), which were to evolve at the cost of the whole organism. Yet once again the Christ being sacrificed himself and "ensouled" himself in an archangel; and likewise once again, in Steiner's account, the powers of this sacrifice benefited the whole human organism on earth and brought about a new harmonization of thinking, feeling, and will. Here in Basel Steiner indicated that mythologies, especially those of ancient Greece, retained a memory of this; and then he passed on to offer a brief reflection on the Mystery of Golgotha itself at the beginning of the Christian era.

Christ had "ensouled" himself three times in the *form of an archangel*; and then, at the beginning of the new era, he assumed corporeal human form without previously dwelling in (or through) an angelic being. In Basel, Steiner was not yet able to say why this was so ("I am obliged to say that I do not know... I must leave it to subsequent enquiries to ascertain why this is so..."), but he emphasizes the importance of the fact. At the beginning of the new era there was no longer the danger of an egoistic and chaotic evolution of the human body or soul (or their organs) induced by adversarial powers, but instead the human individuality and one's incarnational structure as "'I'-organization" was under threat.[25] In the space of a only few words, Rudolf Steiner suggested there was a danger that this "I" would now itself become a "plaything" of powers influencing it from the cosmos and the sphere of the earth elements. Through the incarnation of Christ in Jesus and the three years leading to Golgotha, as well as through the events of Golgotha themselves, this danger was overcome so that not only the human body and soul but also the human "I" was endowed with the capacity for selflessness:

> Our senses have said, Not I but Christ in us. Our life organs have said, Not I but Christ in us. The organs of sensibility have said, Not I but Christ in us. And the human being's moral and intellectual life must also learn to say, Not I but Christ in me.
>
> In three stages, Christ in the suprasensory worlds endowed human beings with the core nature they need if they are to live rightly. In three stages, Christ rendered aspects of human beings selfless—the senses, the life organs, and the organs of sensibility. Now it is up to human beings themselves to become selfless in intellectual and moral ways, learning to comprehend what the phrase "Not I but Christ in me" means in terms of human intellect and morality.

At the end of his lecture on June 1, 1914, Rudolf Steiner went on to describe in exemplary fashion how the Pauline dimension of "Not I but Christ in me" can be present in human culture today and in future, and spoke of our relationship with the dead and the help they can give us for the further work of human individuals on earth. This was just two months after the cremation in Basel of Christian Morgenstern, about whose helping presence Steiner would make very striking comments during the course of 1914.[26] However, on June 1 he was not speaking of Morgenstern's individuality but about Maria von Strauch-Spettini. Dying young, she had taught dramatic arts to Marie von Sivers, and become her close friend, participating intensively in the beginning of anthroposophic work from 1901/02 in Berlin. Later, from the world of spirit, she supported Steiner in the conception and realization of his mystery plays from 1909 onward: "I felt the spiritual power that came to me from without."

As Steiner described this in Basel, he had perceived "the spiritual eye of a spiritual being resting upon what has been undertaken," protecting this work on the mystery plays like a "guardian angel" ("I am describing my direct experience."[27]). The inauguration of the St. John's building on the Dornach hill with a fifth mystery play, originally intended for August 1914, could no longer be realized; difficulties with the building itself, and the outbreak of war, prevented this happening. But the support of Maria von Strauch-Spettini of which Steiner spoke in Basel heralded a new, future cultural epoch in which human beings would develop the capacity of conscious selflessness. When the "I"-nature of those working on earth does not shut itself off selfishly from the world of spirit but has a Pauline relationship to it, the dead can engage with this, and help.

Repeatedly Steiner makes clear that Anthroposophy opens doors to the future, in respect of both method and content:

> If I were to clothe in earthly words what this individuality [Maria von Strauch-Spettini] repeatedly expressed, I would say... "I find such good contact with you because you, for your part, increasingly find ways to make your spiritual science an expression of the living Word of Christ himself."

The building at Dornach, likewise, was to exert a *selfless* effect. Three and a half months after the lecture in Basel, on September 20, 1914—the first anniversary of the laying of the foundation stone—Rudolf Steiner would say at the joinery workshop in Dornach:

> May this outward symbol [the building], even if in a primitive, elementary way, fulfil at least in part what we begged a year ago from the powers of the universe! May people see how the spirit who communed with the earth through the Mystery of Golgotha streams through these forms of ours, takes up these forms and penetrates them with the Christ impulse so that the soul can be pervaded by the awareness that comes to expression in the words, Not I but Christ in me! May this come about for our salvation. May this building, even if it embodies only imperfectly what was intended, to some small degree impress on the human souls who enter here the sense that what strikes my eye through its outward forms does not belong to me myself... but that Christ seeks to speak to me through them; that Christ seeks to come to expression, to revelation through the Word of the higher hierarchies... and that this building is to be his "mouth"![28]

Rudolf Steiner had begun his lecture in Basel by saying that the "school" of Christ was of decisive importance for a future culture of selflessness. He concluded it with words about the future collaboration between the dead and the living:

> The dead unite with the living who understand that Christ found the transition from heavenly to earthly work. And when the dead incline to those alive on earth as their closest protective guardians, they find the souls of those living on earth all the more intensively the more these souls themselves are pervaded and spiritualized by the Christ impulse. Christ descended as sublime sun spirit from supraearthly worlds through the Mystery of Golgotha so that he might find a dwelling in human souls. Spiritual science is to be the message of how Christ can dwell in our souls. When Christ finds his dwelling place in human souls on earth, the Christ strength will shine back from the earth's aura into the worlds from which the Christ departed to redeem earthly humankind, and then the whole cosmos will be Christ-filled.

Two and a half years later, in the middle of World War I, on December 3, 1916, Steiner clarified this further in Zurich, saying:

> An enormous amount would be gained if this selflessness made a little more headway in the world, so that those still alive could connect with the deceased and try to sustain continuity in evolution in a really conscious way. Whether this is based on a purely elective affinity, or some other affinity brought about by karma, connecting with those who seek to send the rays of their influence from the world of spirit is, if we experience it consciously, something of huge significance.[29]

The Basel lecture on June 1, 1914 was the last in a long series of Christological discourses on the so-called Fifth Gospel and the "Preludes to the Mystery of Golgotha," which Steiner had begun in mantric form on September 20, 1913, at the laying of the foundation stone for the Dornach building, and then continued in Norway, Germany, Switzerland, and France until the early summer, shortly before World War I broke out. In this final lecture in Basel, the key motif of Christ's selflessness came to a decisive culmination. At least in the transcript by Rudolf Hahn, Rudolf Steiner's words in other respects were remarkably brief, and he neither described nor named the "archangel being" who was of such key importance in the whole process. In some respects Steiner's lecture in Basel was a summary and—also in relation to the inner processes at work in the Nathan soul—an almost concealing conclusion.[30] Never again, neither during World War I nor in the post-war years through to March 30, 1925, did Steiner ever return to these themes in detail.

The Dornach inauguration of September 20, 1913, with the two foundation stone addresses,[31] had already clearly shown how serious was Steiner's state of mind, and the degree to which he saw the Dornach building project and its spiritual-social objectives as related to the dramatic contemporary situation. Not only did he speak of the "cry of longing for the spirit" in the modern world, and of global anxieties among humankind, but left no doubt as to the spiritual and civilizing power that the School of Spiritual Science in Dornach needed to develop if it were to effectively oppose materialistic-oriented powers of destruction.[32] Directly after the laying of the foundation stone, during which he spoke the "macrocosmic" (reversed) Lord's Prayer for the first time ("The evils hold sway..."), Steiner traveled to Oslo and there, likewise in full awareness of the fraught conditions of the time, began his great account of the "Fifth Gospel." In one of these lectures,[33] most probably to the double astonishment of his audience, he said, "*Humanity must embark upon a conscious grasp of today's events. For this reason we must come to know Christ better, and this is connected with insight into the nature of the human being, Jesus of Nazareth.*" Relating this "conscious grasp of events" to knowledge of Christ—something that was not necessarily self-evident—he then in turn connected this knowledge of Christ to insight into the "human being Jesus of Nazareth." For most of his listeners all this was new, at least in the emphasis he now gave it, even though Steiner had begun to reveal spiritual-scientific secrets of the "human being Jesus of Nazareth" back in September 1909 in Basel.[34] There, after offering some outlines on the theme from the summer of 1909 onward,[35] he had first presented details of the destiny of the "Nathan soul" as he called him, which were to form part of the core of the whole account of the "Fifth Gospel" as this was presented over nine months, and the "Preludes to the Mystery of Golgotha" (from October 1, 1913, to June 1, 1914).

The Nathan soul, the "sister soul of Adam" was the pure, archetypal human being, the epitome of innocence, a being who had never previously incarnated on earth until the time of Christ; and in other words did not participate in the incarnational dynamic of human souls that had been happening since Lemuria. As a solar human soul who did not enter an earthly body he had therefore not succumbed, either, to the earthly influence of anti-Christian adversary powers. ("But when the human "I" descended in Lemurian times into the three sheaths, this being, in a sense as a part of divine human nature, had remained behind in worlds of spirit and had not passed through the evolution of the "I" in these three sheaths, nor its seduction by the luciferic-ahrimanic influx."[36]) This pure soul, possessing unique powers of love and compassion, was born in the Jesus child described by the Gospel of St. Luke, and at the age of twelve united with the "I" of the Zarathustra being (the "essence" with the "image"[37]) subsequently becoming at the age of thirty, following profound experiences, the bearer of the Christ spirit:

> By drawing on what may now be revealed today through true Anthroposophy, it is possible for us to comprehend this kind of intimate reciprocal interplay and union between the Christ being and the human being of the Nathan Jesus.[38]
>
> This is the essential thing about the Mystery of Golgotha—that this being of Jesus, who grew to maturity as the Nathan child, was pervaded by the Christ being.[39]

The unique powers of love, compassion, and, indeed, selflessness possessed by the Nathan Jesus child, were enlarged into the spiritual situation of his surroundings, as Steiner described from October 1913 in his Oslo lectures on the Fifth Gospel, through absorbing the earth-experienced Zarathustra "I," with its knowledge of both earthly and cosmic things.[40] Whereas these powers had, in childhood, related themselves to the Jesus boy's immediate human community, after permeation by the Zarathustra individuality, they oriented themselves to the spiritual situation of the times and from then on were perceived by the Nathan Jesus in their whole apocalyptic drama. According to Rudolf Steiner's lectures from October 1913 onward, the path of Jesus' development up to the Jordan baptism, as the inner foundation for receiving the Christ being at this baptism, was marked by the Nathan Jesus' "despair at the fate of earthly humanity,"[41] and by an "infinite suffering" (*"An...infinite suffering comparable to no suffering on earth that we must ever bear....*"⁴²). Before the Nathan Jesus, says Steiner, no one had been able to perceive in this way *"the degree of intensity that human misery can attain."*⁴³

The whole path of suffering of Jesus of Nazareth on the journey toward the Jordan was by no means a matter of biographical or cultural misery, an experience of violence, war, or catastrophe, but solely one of the decline of spirituality and an awareness of what would ensue from this. The Nathan being, incarnated in Jesus of Nazareth, suffered from the cultural loss of a true image of the human being and the world; experienced, in fact, the whole degenerating incarnation situation of humanity, and anticipated what the future would bring in the coming centuries and millennia if the decline could not be reversed. In this situation the soul longed for a new spiritual influx from the world of spirit, one of *"deep elemental power,"*⁴⁴ a *"macrocosmic illumination of the earth."*⁴⁵ Ultimately this is what occurred in the sacrificial penetration of the Jesus body by the Christ being, enabling the gradual reversal of humanity's decline through a resurrection process.

With his lectures on the Fifth Gospel from October 1913, Rudolf Steiner sought to engender a "living feeling" in his listeners of

> what the Jesus soul had experienced, a sense of the pain of loneliness, the infinite pain.... It is this, a reawakening in ourselves of this suffering, that calls forth in us a living picture of this Christ impulse...as we attempt to make such feelings present within us.⁴⁶

Doubtless he saw a situation arriving at the beginning of the twentieth century that was marked once again by the greatest dramas and enormous approaching suffering. He did not found a School of Spiritual Science in Dornach simply for his anthroposophic friends, but he wished to offer something vital to avert the crises in humanity and potential catastrophes in the fields of education, curative education, medicine, agriculture, as well as in society and politics. He sought to counter the threat to all Creation, and in the face of hugely destructive powers to cultivate the pre-birth and after-death life of the endangered human individuality. The esoteric core of such a "School" could not be established by human powers, not even those of Steiner himself, but must be intended by the spiritual regency of the era *as well as* being deeply sought by human souls, by souls who had experienced the absolute necessity of a new spiritual impulse and *selflessly* longed for this. Two thousand years before, the model or archetype had been given of an existentially necessary renewal of this kind, and, from October 1913, Steiner urged the audience of his Christological lectures to

> gain a picture, one that deeply moves and stirs your souls, of what this human being Jesus of Nazareth had to suffer before he could approach the Mystery of Golgotha so that the Christ impulse could flow into earthly evolution.[47]

In his accounts of the Fifth Gospel, however, he not only described the pain experienced by Jesus up to the time of the Jordan baptism, but also the subsequent three years that he conveyed as a "pressing" of the Christ spirit into the corporeality of Jesus, as the process, from the Jordan baptism onward, whereby the Christ being continued to penetrate the incarnated Nathan soul. In this sense Golgotha signifies the "completion" of the baptism. ("But I have a baptism to be baptized with; and how am I straitened till it be accomplished!" Luke 12:50[48]) Not until Golgotha did the process of incarnation and penetration come to its culmination and completion; there the resurrection body of Christ was prepared, and the decline and degeneration of earthly humanity halted, turning into its opposite.[49] At this point the Christ spirit passed *through pain* into the aura of the earth, as the "Fifth Gospel" taught:

> It will gradually become necessary for humanity to understand that in order to guide earthly evolution from Golgotha onward, this Christ being had to pass through pain to enter the aura of the earth; and that humanity must feel its destiny to be connected with this pain. The connection between humanity and the pain of Christ must grow ever more tangible. Only then will people comprehend how this pain has continued to work in the earth's aura since the Mystery of Golgotha, rejuvenating the powers of earth's evolution.[50]

In countless, harrowing details Rudolf Steiner elaborated all these things from October 1, 1913 onward, calling the Fifth Gospel a "book of power" or a "source of comfort and health."[51] He left no doubt that its content was directly connected with the modern path of selflessness, and possibly was *the* modern book of initiation in an "age of extremes" and in the face of looming evil: "This [the contents of the Fifth Gospel] will be needed in human evolution. The souls who now absorb it will certainly need it for the work that they must perform in the further course of humanity's evolution."[52]

Just as surprising as Steiner's lectures on the Fifth Gospel in Oslo from October 1, 1913, onward,[53] were his accounts of the "preludes" of the Mystery of Golgotha that he began, without any warning, on December 30 1913 at the Hotel de Pologne in Leipzig, in the presence of Christian Morgenstern. Taking up this theme in Stuttgart again shortly afterward and continuing it in various cities (until the conclusion in Basel on June 1, 1914), Steiner described how the Nathan soul, long before the advent of Christ, had shared in the destiny of earthly humanity and experienced its suffering while he still dwelt in cosmic heights. Though this soul's first incarnation had occurred roughly 2,000 years ago, it had begun to engage far, far earlier in an existential connection with the plight of earthly and human evolution, and since then had been an inner participant in it.

What Rudolf Steiner summarized and concluded in Basel on June 1, 1914, eight weeks before the outbreak of war, had been successively elaborated from December 30, 1913, onward. And in Leipzig, from the very beginning, reference had been made to the Nathan being who, de facto, was the *archangel* or *archangel-like* being whom Christ had previously sacrificially penetrated on three occasions.[54] According to the Fifth Gospel, the Nathan being "sacrificed" himself at the Jordan to enable the Christ spirit and Christ impulse to stream into earthly evolution. But this sacrifice was one the same soul had already previously engaged in on three previous occasions. All three sacrifices before the time of Christ had endowed human evolution on earth with an influx of powers. Only with the final completion of the Jordan sacrifice at Golgotha had these powers been reversed so that they could now stream back out from the earth into the cosmos and initiate a process that was still far from finished in the twentieth century—as Steiner explained in a profound essay ("What is the Earth in Reality in the Macrocosm?"[55]).

~

From December 30, 1913, onward, Rudolf Steiner described the three cosmic "preludes" to the Mystery of Golgotha in aspects and details that no longer figured in the summarizing Basel account and the theme of selflessness with which it culminated. At the anthroposophic branch on Stuttgart's Landhausstrasse, in March 1914, for instance, he first explained that the Nathan soul—while still dwelling "on the sun" in the Lemurian era—heard the plight of the human senses crying up for help to worlds of spirit—the "lament and cry for help" or the "cry of pain of tormented humanity."[56] These words are reminiscent of the foundation stone mantras of September 20, 1913, as well as accounts from the Fifth Gospel concerning the situation of Jesus of Nazareth, the Nathan soul, at the time of Christ.

According to Steiner, these cries of pain "drove" the Nathan soul "toward the sun spirit" at the time of ancient Lemuria,[57] in the same way that Jesus of Nazareth was "driven" much later toward the Jordan and to the Christ-permeation that occurred there. ("The 'I' of Zarathustra had withdrawn and there now lived in his three sheaths only what had remained behind through the power of his experiences. Within these three sheaths an impulse now came to the fore, driving him upon a path that led him toward John the Baptist at the River Jordan."[58]) The inner suffering undergone by the Nathan being on the sun in experiencing the "lament of the human senses" or the "cry of pain of tormented humanity" affected and changed this soul so that—as Steiner said in Leipzig—it became a vessel fit to be permeated by the Christ.[59] Similarly, the soul-spiritual sufferings of Jesus of Nazareth were the necessary condition for him to receive the sun-spirit Christ at the Jordan baptism.

The first sacrificing interpenetration of the Christ Being and the Nathan soul, as Steiner had already explained in Leipzig, attenuated the human sensory organism and formative powers from the cosmos that stream into the earth in a twelvefold way from the zodiac. ("On Old Saturn, the sensory organs were first created as seeds of the physical body, as reflections of the twelve cosmic streams emanating from the sublime spiritual beings of the first hierarchy, and coming to outward expression in the twelvefold zodiac" Prokofieff.[60]) The excessive excitability or "hypersensibility" (or "hypersensitivity")[61] of the luciferically impregnated and instigated senses was thus taken from them. In various lectures, including the one in Leipzig where these things were first mentioned, Rudolf Steiner also stated that the intended deformation of human sensory processes (toward a "selfish" hypersensitivity) was not the result of purely luciferic but combined luciferic-ahrimanic influence: "We can say that the worst effects of Lucifer and Ahriman were repulsed from the human senses by higher worlds [through the Christ sacrifice]."[62] Summarizing this first remedial measure by the cosmos to save the human being, Steiner said in Munich on March 30, 1914, one day before his friend Christian Morgenstern died: "The nature of our twelve senses became what it did because Christ sank himself into the soul of the one who would later be the Nathan Jesus, and assuaged the human sensory system."[63]

This first permeation of the Nathan soul by Christ also had consequences for the Nathan soul itself. Having until then possessed the "form of an angel," the Christ sacrifice of permeation endowed this soul with "etheric human form," as Rudolf Steiner first (and uniquely) explained in Pforzheim on March 9, 1814.[64] After the sacrificial deed accomplished in the realm of the sun,[65] the power of the "etheric, supraearthly Christ being" henceforth inherent in the Nathan soul, streamed with physical sun radiance toward the earth and toward the "physical earth form" of human beings. This not only changed the structure of the senses but, via the body-*constituting* influence of the sensory sphere, also our whole corporeality:

> Thus something new penetrated the cosmos, radiating to the earth and making it possible for the human being, the physical earth form of the human being, into whom streamed the power of the etheric suprasensory Christ being, to safeguard himself against the destruction that would inevitably have occurred if the configuring power that allows him to become a properly ordered, upright being had not shone in from the cosmos and penetrated him, thus living in him. Disorder would inevitably have arisen if with the physical sunlight there had not streamed in that forming, configuring power that can shine in because of this first Christ event. What the human being received into himself in consequence has lived in humanity's evolution since the time of ancient Lemuria.[66]

In this brief outline, Rudolf Steiner was pointing to very significant occurrences. The spirit form of the physical body (the "phantom") was strengthened through this first sacrifice of Christ and the Nathan soul, and safeguarded from premature destruction. At the same time, through the instreaming power of the "etheric suprasensory Christ being," human beings were endowed with the power to raise themselves upright, which, in the last evolutionary period of "ancient Lemuria," sundered them (with the help of the Spirits of Form) from earthly powers, and allowed them to become upright, walking creatures:

> At the moment when the child stands upright, and no longer crawling or sliding along awkwardly, stands or walks for the first time, we can properly understand the developing human child if we see that this can happen only in

a way befitting humanity's proper development and salvation because the first Christ event occurred in ancient Lemurian times; and because the Nathan Jesus who later permeated himself with Christ, was in those Lemurian times a spiritual-etheric being who, through permeation by Christ, took on human-etheric form.[67]

In his series on the "Preludes to the Mystery of Golgotha," given before the final lecture in Basel, Steiner also spoke in more detail about the second interpenetration of the Christ being and the Nathan soul. In his account, this second sacrifice no longer occurred on the sun but, as part of a successive approach to the earth by *both* the Christ being and the Nathan soul, in the planetary region instead. This cosmic sphere, as Steiner repeatedly emphasized in relation to the nature and constitution of the human being, is at the same time the source from which the human organism's life organs draw their "founding etheric forces." Here dwelt the Nathan soul in the early period of Atlantean evolution, "most deeply moved within" by experiencing how the luciferic-ahrimanic powers were inducing an "abnormal development" of the life forces, and were in the process of letting the human being's organic state, formerly ordered with great wisdom, degenerate into "greed and revulsion." In Leipzig already, Steiner said of this:

> And behold, the same being who later appeared in the Nathan Jesus child, who...had formerly lived upon the sun and had there been spiritualized by the Christ being, the sublime sun being, now moved from planet to planet, most deeply moved within by the impossibility of allowing human evolution to continue as it was. So strong was the

effect of this experience upon this being as it incarnated upon one planet after another, that Christ once again permeated it at a certain point during Atlantean evolution.[68]

Permeation by the Christ spirit "at a certain point during Atlantean evolution" once again led to "strength radiating into the earth aura." Once again there was a therapeutic intervention from the cosmos, though this time connected with the sevenfold nature of the planets rather than the twelvefold zodiac.[69] The resulting reconfiguration of the life organs in their nature and functional interplay changed the human being's physiological situation such that the further evolution of his speech became possible above and beyond organically determined or dominated sentient utterances—as Steiner first described this in Pforzheim on March 7, 1914. In this way the human being became not only an upright, standing, and walking being but also the bearer of a capacity of speech that limits and transcends our organic existence. In consequence we later became capable (through further evolution) of "selflessly" identifying or perceiving objective realities. But these developments, later counted among "self-evident" human accomplishments, were preceded by dramatic battles and conflicts.

Likewise in these Christological lectures prior to Basel, Steiner spoke of the third interpenetration of Christ and the Nathan soul. This, he said, took place in the earth's immediate vicinity as the new era and the Mystery of Golgotha drew nearer. The Nathan being, said Steiner in Leipzig, had by this point assumed a "cosmic soul form" such that

> his life was now neither on the earth, nor the moon, nor the sun but, as if circling the earth, felt itself dependent on the influences of sun, moon and earth all at once. The earthly influences rose up to him from below, while those of the

moon and the sun descended from above. Clairvoyant awareness sees this being, if I can put it like this, in the flower of his development at this time, and in the same sphere in which the moon orbits the earth. Therefore, I cannot exactly say that the moon influence came from above since it emanated really from the place where he himself was, this pre-earthly Nathan Jesus. Once again there cried up to him what human thinking, feeling and will would inevitably have become, and within himself he sought to fully experience and feel this tragedy of humanity's evolution. But because of this he once again called down to him the lofty sun spirit who now settled upon him, spiritualizing him for the third time.[70]

Here again Steiner emphasized not only the secret of the sacrifice and interpenetration as such but also what led to it and caused it. The Nathan soul did not merely passively witness the suffering of human evolution, but *intentionally* sought to "fully experience" it; and only through this did the next step become possible (consisting in the gathering and transformation of sun, moon, and earth forces, as the macrocosmic equivalents of microcosmic thinking, feeling, and will, and in the union with the Christ being). Only through the inner processes and deeds of the Nathan Soul was it once more possible for the Christ sun spirit to accomplish his sacrifice and perform the necessary "soul-permeation." On March 5, 1914, in Stuttgart, Steiner first indicated the degree to which the innocent, pure Nathan "spirit being" had in this case to share compassionately in human suffering:

> The spirit being had to immerse itself in the human soul that was brimful with passions, had itself to become these passions, become a dragon, in order to transform the soul forces and, for a third time, to let itself be illumined by the Christ spirit.[71]

The "ennobling" of the dragon thereby accomplished, reflected in myth and legend in the battle of Michael or St. George with the dragon, and the subsequent Christ sacrifice, once again sent shining influences to the earth, or in other words signified a renewed cosmic-therapeutic intervention in the evolving human organism. Here a triad was decisive, encompassing sun, moon, and earth; thinking, feeling, and will were reoriented to each other, preparing to receive a further principle, the unity of the "I," which would become ever more apparent as evolution continued. For its forthcoming arrival the "I" needed a harmoniously ordered soul organism. Connected with this was a finer development of the human speech organs and the human capacity for speech, which from then on increasingly acquired the ability to "name" the world, as Rudolf Steiner stressed in March 1914 in Pforzheim:

> Then a third Christ event occurred. For the third time the being in spirit heights who would later be born as the Nathan Jesus united with the Christ being and, with the powers it had now assumed, poured itself into the human capacity for speech. The power of this Christ–Jesus being thus penetrated organs in the human body for a second time; the organs employed in speech and utterance. This made it possible for speech to create true signs for the outer environment, so that it could become a means of communication across diverse regions of humanity. A child could never learn to speak if these two Christ events had not occurred in Atlantean times. And we enrich our sense of things, our feelings, through spiritual science if, as a child begins to speak, and increasingly perfects this ability, we remember that Christ impulses hold sway within it—that the power of Christ lives in speech in a protecting and nurturing way.[72]

On June 1, 1914, in Basel, Rudolf Steiner spoke no more than a few sentences about the Mystery of Golgotha itself and the "redemption" of the human "I," indicating that the fourth Christ sacrifice, the permeation of the Nathan soul on earth, averted the danger of "chaotic" "I"-development at that turning point of time. In previous years he had repeatedly spoken of the significance of the deed at Golgotha and the creation of the resurrection body for the preservation and further evolution of the human being on earth. He did this in greatest detail in the course he gave in the autumn of 1911 in Karlsruhe, which was entitled *From Jesus to Christ*.[73] But the prime aspects on which he focused in his series on the "preludes" to the Mystery of Golgotha, were not, or at least not primarily, about the creation of the resurrection body but were concerned rather with the threat to the "I" itself; they related to the "I"-governed capacity for thinking that had become possible in the evolution of consciousness toward the time of Christ owing to the reordered human body and soul. The human being had become an upright, speaking, and—increasingly—thinking being. And connected with this capacity for thinking was the means to develop "I"-consciousness, against which ahrimanic and luciferic powers were battling with all their might.

In many of his Christological lectures since the foundation stone was laid in September 1913, Rudolf Steiner had spoken of these things in much greater detail than he did on June 1, 1914, in Basel. He also included certain aspects of these accounts in the new two-volume edition of *Riddles of Philosophy* (1914), originally published as *Nineteenth-Century Views of the World and Life*. In the first chapter of this book ("The Worldview of Greek Thinkers") Steiner pointed to the "appearance of an independent experience of thought" in the last five pre-Christian centuries in ancient Greece. Drawing on developments in philosophy he sought to show that due to a "transformation in the subtler human organism" a former pictorial or picturing capacity had been extinguished by the developing power of thought, giving rise in its place to a new self-perception of the human being as a thinking being. The human soul, as he described it in this "exoteric" book intended for the general public, became aware of itself and its thinking powers. It began to grasp and comprehend itself, gaining an increasing sense of its autonomy and inner coherence.[74] Steiner also spoke of these processes in Christological lectures centered on the evolution of human consciousness, which were given at the same time as this chapter was written. "A quite different kind of worldview arose in the sixth century BC, an entirely new epoch.... This becomes very clear to us if we carefully study these times."[75] A "radical reconfiguration of the thought world of humanity through centuries" occurred in ancient Greece in preparation for the dawn of the new era—a phenomenal degree of "deepening thought" signifying entirely new territory both for humanity and for cultural history:

> Whatever we may initially believe, thought had never existed in this way before, in no other nation, and in no other time![76]
>
> Something happens to thought, which approaches the human soul, in a sense, in a way quite different from ever before...[77]

In both written and verbal form in 1913/14, Steiner described this radical new departure in consciousness in very striking ways, showing how it arose with the appearance of the first Greek natural philosophers surrounding Heraclitus,

Thales, and others. Inspired by the archangel Michael, who prepared this new development, guiding culture and spiritual evolution toward the era of Christ, the human soul began a life in ideas. Over centuries it accomplished an "infinitely significant elaboration of worlds of ideas," in this process developing trust in thinking and in the "formulation of concepts and ideas."[78] This was a preparation for the influx of the "I," which increasingly approached the human being and would ultimately enter him, "awakening" through and in the human body, and thus coming to earthly "birth." The whole of Greek philosophy is a "significant expression of the birth of the 'I,'" said Rudolf Steiner in a lecture on the Fifth Gospel in Berlin on February 10, 1914.[79]

But this process, too, did not occur without hindrance. On December 29, 1913, in Leipzig, Steiner first described the powers of the "sibyls" who emerged parallel to the early Greek philosophers and massively endangered the intended developments. From the eighth century BC, as he said in Leipzig and in subsequent Christological lectures, prophecies had emerged in Greece from "curious," "chaotic" subterranean regions of the human soul. These were mediumistic soul-forces which, far removed from "ordered thinking," had surfaced in humanity with "spiritualized fanaticism," forcefully imposing their "messages." Even the earliest Greek philosophers in Ionia, according to Steiner, tried to oppose "chaos" with "clear, bright, and light-filled ideas," seeking in fact to establish a "philosophy of clarity" and to manifest the "spirit through the 'I.'" In radical polarity to this, the shadowy spirit emanations of the sibyls worked out of "soul chaos." They drew sustenance from elemental earth forces ("If, through spiritual science, we study where the powers of the sibyls originate, we have to say that they flow from what we can call the spiritual powers of the earth itself, which are connected more with the subterranean regions of the human soul"[80]) and also absorbed external influences from their immediate location. Steiner spoke here of a spiritual "atavism" and the very mixed nature of their oracular utterances which contained things that were true but also grotesquely false ("sometimes great pearls of wisdom for the future"—"lunatic things"). This only further heightened their seductive powers:

> We see that these sibyls' prophetic statements could be true and beneficent, but that on the other hand, speaking out of disordered "I" powers, they could sow misunderstanding and deceitfulness.[81]

According to Rudolf Steiner, the Greek philosophers, as well as the Hebrew prophets, worked for the future of humanity's evolution, for its thought and "I"-development, in accordance with Michael and the approaching Christ. The Christ being, the "'I' of worlds" and the "higher human 'I'" continued to approach closer to the realm of earth so as to unite with the destiny of humanity and each individual. As Steiner said in Munich on March 30, 1914, both the Greek philosophers and the Hebrew prophets were "preparing the Christ impulse; in pure, inner contemplation they sought to absorb the young Christ power, and to experience what is at work in humanity's evolution in an ordered life of thought."[82] They tried "to calm the 'I'" or, in view of the massive interferences, to "introduce order again into "I" powers."[83] But neither the Hebrew prophets nor the Greek philosophers were ultimately able to prevent the "I"-chaos instigated by the (luciferic–ahrimanic) forces standing behind the figures of the sibyls. Steiner says that "spiritual chaos" was looming in Western culture and far beyond, in ways that would destroy or entirely occlude the "clarity of the 'I'" that had been achieved in the centuries of Christ's approach to the earth.

> And if we ask ourselves how this was averted, and who ensured that this power we perceive so tangibly living in the sibyls was gradually attenuated, we must reply that it was Christ who flowed out into the earth's aura through the Mystery of Golgotha, and who destroyed the power of the sibyls, removed the sibylline power, *within and out of human souls*.[84]
>
> If it had not been for the Mystery of Golgotha, the sibylline element would have been victorious over conscious "I" powers, would have suppressed them. The "I" would have been lost to human evolution.[85]

> The order *proclaimed* in advance by the teachings of the prophets was created by the Mystery of Golgotha; "I" powers were ordered in a way that enabled the human to learn ever more profoundly, Not I but Christ in me.... The event of Golgotha had to occur on earth because it is on earth that the human "I" must evolve.[86]

The Christ being, said Steiner in the months before the beginning of World War I—a time that was itself strongly marked by spiritual conflicts and the clouding of consciousness[87]—led the spiritual battle with the sibyls; he fulfilled his "judging" role and, through this "metaphysical deed," accomplished "unending things for humanity."[88]

Rudolf Steiner did not speak explicitly in this context about the Nathan soul incarnated in Jesus of Nazareth. In his lectures on the Fifth Gospel, however, he described not only the disconcerting experiences this soul underwent in relation to the spiritual impotence of contemporary Judaism, but also his despair at the distortions of ancient mysteries and their practices, which were now inhabited by demons. It was here that Jesus of Nazareth first heard the "reversed Lord's Prayer": "The evils hold sway..."[89] Doubtless these processes were not primarily the signs of outward decline but were connected with the occult battles characterized by Steiner in relation to the sibyls, which engulfed the old mystery sites also. In this situation, the Nathan soul's absolute longing for "macrocosmic illumination" was directed toward the approaching Christ being as solar "universal 'I,'" with whom he wished to unite on earth for the redemption of humankind. An ordering of the "I"—inwardly and in its relationship to the surrounding world—along with the necessary further evolution of thinking, of "healthy thinking in accord with truth,"[90] was possible only through the appearance of the Christ sun being *on earth*, within a bodily human organism.

Implicit in the reversal of the macrocosmic Lord's Prayer was the "I" and its new order; this became possible through the incarnation event at the Jordan baptism, as the fourth sacrifice of both Christ and the Nathan soul, a sacrifice which continued until the events on the hill of Golgotha and only then came to final fulfillment. Only then, as Rudolf Steiner described it, was the incarnational descent of the Christ being into Jesus of Nazareth completed; only then did he fully penetrate the body of Jesus, right into his bones. Steiner said nothing about the length of time taken by the three first sacrificial deeds of Christ and the Nathan soul; the fourth sacrifice, the fourth "penetration" however, took place over a period of three years, and heralded the order of the "I."

After the Nathan soul, incarnated in the man Jesus of Nazareth, had entirely absorbed the Christ being, every single human "I" could henceforth gain access to him and his impulses. This also meant that human thinking could finally and fully unite with the "I" and thus continue the process that had begun many centuries before but, prior to the Mystery of Golgotha, had been gravely endangered. On March 7, 1914, in Pforzheim, Steiner "translated" the prologue to the St. John's Gospel as follows:

> In the beginning is the thought
> And the thought is with God,
> And a God is the thought.
> In it is life
> And the life is to become the light of my "I."
> And may the divine thought shine into my "I,"
> So that this divine thought comprehend and encompass
>   The darkness of my "I."[91]

What subsequently unfolded over almost two millennia was an enduring battle for human thinking or the destiny of intelligence. Michael, as Steiner described him, had "administered" this intelligence as cosmic asset through long periods of time, but, following the Mystery of Golgotha, and the "redemption of the human capacity of individual 'I'-thinking" (Prokofieff) associated with it, had sacrificed it over many centuries, making it available to the human being on earth.[92] Much had altered by the time Michael was at last able to influence earthly events again as "time spirit" in 1879. The intelligence originally governed by him had by then passed almost entirely to human beings, who were now able to think through the instrument of the "I" and, in the thinking process, become aware of their active "I." At the same time, though, they were striding ever further into earthly matter and into Ahriman's force field. Residing with God "in the beginning," the thought itself—whose life and divine nature was perceived and increasingly encompassed by the human being's soul-spiritual organization—had also embarked on a descent into the earthly world. It was now being wholly shaped within the human physical body and experienced there, too, in its unreal, mirror-image nature. Ten years after his Basel lecture on the four sacrifices of Christ, Rudolf Steiner wrote:

> As thoughts took hold of the physical body, spirit, soul and life were expunged from their immediate content; and only the abstract shadow remained, adhering to the physical body. Such thoughts can only enquire into physical, material subjects, for they themselves are only real within the confines of the human being's physical-material body.[93]

> As thoughts pass over into the physical body they lose their living quality. They become dead, spiritually dead configurations. Previously they belonged to the human being as organs, also, of divine, spiritual beings to whom the human being belongs. Within the human being they had *essential will*. And because of this, one felt connected through them with the living world of spirit. With dead thoughts, one feels detached from the spiritual world, entirely translated into the physical world, and thus into the sphere of ahrimanic spirituality.[94]

> The physical organism is the grave of living thinking, the container of such thinking.[95]

With thoughts as "dead shadows of the spirit" humanity was, since the beginning of modern times, slipping with increasing rapidity into a "different world history." World

War I, on the eve of which Steiner spoke about Christ's sacrifice in Basel, was doubtless connected with this outline of evolution, and was itself part of a "different world history." Progressive materialization in various walks of life had consequences and was connected closely with the modes of thinking of social Darwinism, eugenics, ethnic cleansing, nationalism, and imperialism. Indeed, these testified to a common origin in the history of human consciousness with its distortion of the image of the human being. According to Steiner, materialistic thinking had culminated back in the 1840s, seventy years before World War I, as can be evidenced by many aspects of the history of science in the nineteenth century.[96]

These developments had not only placed great obstacles in the way of the new Michael age and the regency of Michael—sometimes even making it seem impossible for this age to dawn—but also had grave consequences for the world of spirit, at least in regard to the earth's spiritual aura. Thirteen months before his Basel lecture on the Christ being's four sacrifices and the Nathan soul, as well as the Christ culture of selflessness, Steiner spoke in London for the first time about Christ in the materialistic nineteenth century, and the Nathan soul connected with him. This was on May 2, 1913. However, he did not mention the Nathan soul by name there, only describing how Christ since Golgotha revealed himself in an "angelic being" as his outward figure and form. In the course of the nineteenth century, this angelic being had—because of materialistic thinking, feeling, and willing that the dead carried with them into the world of spirit as a "black sphere of materialism"—undergone an "extinction" of his consciousness, suffering a kind of "death by suffocation." Steiner gave no precise details of this suffocation but the whole thrust of his account showed that this was not a final "death" in the earthly sense but instead a qualitative change of limited duration. ("There are conditions in which consciousness experiences a grim isolation in the world of spirit, and of sporadic immersion in something like sleep, but death does not exist in the higher worlds. Death is impossible there."[97])

The (temporary) "destruction" of the consciousness of the angelic being, whose preceding torments Steiner did not describe, was caused by a deed of Christ, who had decided to take up the "black sphere of materialism" into his own being (and thus also that of the angelic being so closely connected with him) so as to be able to transform them. Steiner spoke here of a sacrifice of Christ that was comparable to the Mystery of Golgotha, and must be regarded as a "second crucifixion" in the etheric realm. But this sacrifice, like the one preceding it at the dawn of the new era, affected not only the Christ being himself but also this close angelic companion, whom we can discern, through his mission for humanity and proximity to Christ, as the Nathan soul. Sergei Prokofieff wrote, "In the whole of human evolution there is no being who was, is and will remain so profoundly and intensely connected with Christ both on earth and in the spiritual cosmos."[98]

On May 20, 1913, in referring to these things once more (this time in Stuttgart) Steiner spoke of the Christ (and the angelic soul) being "driven out" from the world of spirit by a "conspiracy" of materialistic souls:

> And the efforts made by these souls who had crossed the threshold succeeded in driving Christ out (we can use no other word) from the world of spirit. The Christ was compelled to undergo a renewal of the Mystery of Golgotha, albeit not to the same degree as formerly. Then he had

passed through death, but now he was expelled from his existence in the spiritual world.[99]

Christ, with the Nathan soul, was driven out of the spiritual worlds and translated into the sensory world, "that of humankind," not in the form of a new incarnation but in an intensified presence there. Since this new sacrifice—de facto the fifth—by the Christ being and the Nathan soul (very probably the *first* since the Mystery of Golgotha), Christ, as Steiner emphasized in 1913, has been united with the destiny of human beings on earth in a "still more intimate way." Since then, with increasing intensity, the Christ consciousness previously concealed can *"flare up again to live in human souls on earth."*[100] In his studies on the Fifth Gospel, Andreas Neider stressed that the extinguishing of Christ consciousness in the spiritual world signified that the Christ being lost awareness of his own history—i.e., a memory of his connection with the Nathan soul, and that it had been Rudolf Steiner's initiate mission at the beginning of the apocalyptic twentieth century to reverse this process:

> Rudolf Steiner drew from the Akashic records the memories of Jesus of Nazareth, humanity's sister soul, and the prelude to the Mystery of Golgotha in which Christ united with this sister soul in the body of Jesus of Nazareth. Thus he brought this to his own awareness and that of his listeners. By so doing, the consciousness of Christ Jesus himself begins to reawaken. Christ consciousness begins to reawaken through what was accomplished just in time before the outbreak of World War I in Rudolf Steiner and the people surrounding him and working with him.[101]

In one of his lectures on the Fifth Gospel (on December 18, 1913, in Cologne) Steiner hinted that to enquire into these circumstances, and thus to facilitate the rekindling of a "previously concealed Christ consciousness in human souls on earth," he had in a certain sense to sacrifice his consciousness to the time spirits of the archai (and first and foremost to the *archē* Michael). "Higher research," he said, "is not possible without inner tragedy, inner suffering."[102] The biography of Steiner's life and work at this period bears a distinctive tone;[103] and the laying of the foundation stone in Dornach, as well as the whole Goetheanum building, were connected with this process of awakening Christ consciousness among humankind,[104] and *for this reason* involved bitter conflict from the very beginning.

—

Rudolf Steiner did not describe what the Nathan soul, so closely allied with humanity's suffering, underwent in the nineteenth century prior to and during the sacrifice and temporary death process, the "destruction" or "extinguishing" of this soul's consciousness; he remained silent about the "cries" the soul may have once again heard before sacrificing itself again and succumbing to unconsciousness. He did however comment on the situation of Michael during the rise of scientific materialism (with the euphoric transposition of its scientific methodology and partial discoveries to the humanities) during the first two-thirds of the nineteenth century. Writing at the end of 1924, a few months before his death, he said of this period:

> [During the nineteenth century] one can observe Michael with great concern, seeing that he is as yet unsure whether he will be able to combat the "dragon" in the long term, since he perceives how human beings seek to gain an image of the human from their newly obtained picture of nature

in the field of science. Michael sees how human beings regard nature and how they wish to create an image of the human being from what they call "natural laws." He sees how people picture humankind arising from increasingly perfected animal qualities, from evolving organs. But no "human being" arises in this way before the spirit of eye of Michael since what is pictured as evolving and being harmonized in this way is only "thought"; no one can perceive any such evolution in reality, since this is not at all what happens. Thus human beings live with such ideas about humankind in unreal pictures, in illusions; they hunt for an image of the human being that they only think they possess. In reality, their field of vision is empty. What Michael says of this, in fearful concern, can be heard as Inspiration roughly in these words: "The strength of the spiritual sun shines upon their souls; Christ works upon them. But as yet they remain unaware of it. The strength of the consciousness soul holds sway in their body but as yet does not find entry to the soul."

It remains a question whether the power of illusion in human beings may give the dragon sufficient might to thwart Michael's efforts to hold the balance.... Michael's preparation of his mission for the end of the nineteenth century appears to unfold in cosmic tragedy. Below on the earth people often experience profoundest satisfaction at the efficacy of their image of nature; but in the realm where Michael works, tragedy prevails in respect of the hindrances that oppose the development of a true image of the human being. Formerly Michael's austere love lived in the rays of the sun, in the shimmering colors of dawn, in the shining of the stars; now this love had become most strongly imbued with a tone of suffering in its perception of humanity. Michael's situation in the cosmos became a tragic and difficult one, yet nevertheless was urgently seeking a solution precisely in the period preceding his mission for the earth.[105]

Thus Steiner spoke of a "tone of suffering" in Michael's perception of humanity. But assuredly the situation for the "sister soul of Adam" and companion of Christ (closely associated with Michael[106]) appeared a great deal more dramatic, for this soul took up into itself and bore all human suffering, once more in relation to the forthcoming *consequences* of contemporary developments. At the turning point of time, Jesus of Nazareth had suffered unimaginable torments in his concern for humanity. Steiner remained silent about the inner situation of the Nathan soul amidst the spiritual drama of the nineteenth century. During the course of the twentieth century, millions of human souls were to suffer "death by suffocation" (in the gas chambers) in their millions, as the victims of a scientific picture of the human being and its totalitarian realization in nationalism, racism, eugenics, and anti-Semitism. They, and subsequent victims of mechanization, technology, and human manipulation—right into diverse organs and human DNA—were preceded by the Nathan soul in the sphere of consciousness.

Since the second Mystery of Golgotha, the Christ being (and the Nathan soul with him) is still more "intimately" united with the destiny of humanity, as Steiner stressed in London, one of the imperial strongholds of modern science and technology, on May 2, 1913, the year before war broke out. This "intimate" connection of Christ with humanity will become increasingly apparent in future in human beings' experiences of Christ, as he also explained in other Christological accounts he gave before World War I. Such experiences, however, would especially occur through human distress and misery:[107]

Christ will stand beside the human being and offer him counsel. This is not meant only as an image but as reality; people will receive the advice they need from the living Christ, who will be their counselor and friend, speaking to human souls like someone who walks physically beside us. (Oct. 14, 1913[108])

The mighty deed of sacrifice by Christ, and the Nathan being connected with him, the second "crucifixion" in the etheric, formed the basis for a new "Christ consciousness" to arise in the human being. The Christ will be able to approach human beings more closely in future *because* they will increasingly find their way to him and the Nathan soul, in the further evolution of consciousness, by passing through spiritual abysses: "Only a few to begin with, but in the course of the twentieth century increasing numbers will be able to perceive the appearance of the etheric Christ, that is, Christ in the form of an angel."[109] In future, Steiner also said on March 7, 1914, in Pforzheim,[110] the Christ will approach human beings "as an angel-like being," that is in union with the Nathan soul.[111]

> Thus find in decline
> And in death's night
> Creation's new beginning,
> Morning's strong, new light.[112]

In his Christological reflections, and in other lectures and writings, Steiner connected both the direction of "decline" into the "night of death" and the "new beginning" very closely with the destiny of human intelligence and human thought. His whole spiritual-scientific work was based on a "resurrection" of thinking and thus also on reversal of the process that had culminated in the nineteenth century in the "death of thinking" as has been described, in the "grave" of the physical body. In the human being this formed the basis of all outward processes of destruction. On May 2, 1913, in London, Steiner spoke not only of a repetition of the Mystery of Golgotha in the etheric sphere in the nineteenth century but also of a Michael-inspired, spiritual knowledge and science of the future, "which as yet is only just beginning." [113] Michael became the "ambassador" of Christ and, according to Steiner in his lecture in London, will in forthcoming centuries grant seekers wide-reaching "spiritual revelations" that successively reveal the Mystery of Golgotha:

> Michael can give us new spiritual light, which we can regard as a transformation of the light given through him at the time of the Mystery of Golgotha; and the people of our time may place themselves into this light. If we can feel this, then we can comprehend the whole significance of the new age that is emerging from our own in the present day. We can discern the dawning of a spiritual revelation that is to enter the life of humanity on earth in the next few centuries. Indeed, since humanity has become freer than it once was, we will be able, through our own will, to progress in a way that enables us to receive this revelation.[114]

What Rudolf Steiner presented as the Fifth Gospel in Oslo from October 1913 onward, together with further aspects of the Mystery of Golgotha apparent in his lectures on the "preludes" to this mystery, between December 30, 1913, and June 1, 1914, doubtless belonged to the gifts of Michael to which he referred in London.

As such, however, they had an inherent connection with Rudolf Steiner's spiritual-scientific path of research, centered as this was on the active, "I"-governed thinking process that releases itself from the "grave" of the physical body. Modern and future seekers on this path are granted "spiritual revelations." Immediately on his return from London, in May 1913, Steiner spoke in Stuttgart about "active" and "passive" thinking. He described the latter as being directly dependent on the brain, bringing to consciousness only thoughts "reflected" in the brain. ("Then this thinking is more passive, is a kind of thinking that wishes to rely on the instrument of the brain."[115]) He continued:

> Or instead this thinking can quite simply—without any kind of meditation—liberate itself by inwardly collecting itself, which it does by becoming aware of its true nature and seeking to sunder itself from such reliance on the brain. Then it becomes a more active thinking. Both are aspects of healthy human thinking as every soul can practice it today. Every soul can think, but this thinking can be used in two ways; initially we can strengthen our faculties and inwardly form thoughts.... But if this thinking does not seek to strengthen itself, does not wish to grasp itself in independent activity, then it has to rely instead on the brain as instrument of thinking, and then it will only produce thoughts that are encompassed by this instrument of the brain. In this case a person is thinking passively rather than actively. More important than almost anything else (though not for the immediate present but for the future) is discernment of the difference between active and passive thinkers.[116]

In his very last lecture course before the war began, in Norrköping, Sweden, in July 1914, entitled *Christ and the Human Soul*, Steiner spoke among other things of the need in the modern age to develop Christ consciousness in the face of devastating events. We could, he said, hold in our mind a picture of the (first) crucifixion of Christ in terms of the fact that the being who first makes us truly human and at the same time gives "goal and meaning" to the earth had been put to death. A fundamental darkening of perception of the true essence of the human being occurred in spiritual and cultural history through an over-incarnational process[117] (described in the "reversed" Lord's Prayer), and humanity lost the capacity to (re)discover its essential nature by its own powers. In this situation, true self-knowledge could only be gained by separation from the physical body, which is why all mystery centers of the past worked with this in view. But as Steiner elaborated in Norrköping, the Mystery of Golgotha rekindled the powers that had been lost in humanity's evolution, most essentially in the realm of thinking, which now became available for "Christ-permeation."

The macrocosmic Lord's Prayer, which relates to the "secret of the whole human embodiment in physical, earthly corporeality" was radically reversed by Christ,[118] making it possible for us to reconnect anew with the cosmos: "He knew that the human being must, from below upward, now seek the path into worlds of spirit,"[119] that is, toward increasing liberation of the powers of soul and spirit from the body. The last chapter of Steiner's book, *Riddles of Philosophy*, starts precisely here with its outlook on the future. Steiner wrote it in a few days in Berlin four weeks after the war began, at the end of August 1914,[120] and shortly after his conversation with Helmuth von Moltke in Niederlahnstein.[121] This chapter concerned the need for developing an intensified experience of thinking activity, liberating it from dependency on the body, and in other words condensing and intensifying it so that it can be "reflected" and thus come to awareness, through and in itself. On September 1, 1914, in the foreword to the second edition of the book, Steiner emphasized that this involved the soul—in thinking—becoming able to experience its own spiritual essence and making this conscious in a way that was independent of experience and perception of the world of the senses. Thus it would also be independent of the physical instrument of the body.

In his pre-war lectures on the Fifth Gospel and the preludes to the Mystery of Golgotha, Rudolf Steiner repeatedly spoke of the necessity of this for creating a real future in the evolution of consciousness and the whole of civilization. Human thinking, at risk before the advent of Christ, and redeemed by Christ's incarnation in its "I"-informed and "I"-governed order and clarity, can and must seed our future evolution. The Christ impulse can enter and inform this thinking in so far as the human being succeeds in developing it further in a selfless, body-free way and offering it up to the world of spirit and its revelations.

In his Christological lectures, and also in the final chapter of *The Riddles of Philosophy,* Steiner returned again and again to the picture of the grain of corn; this can be used as food or can be allowed to develop its inner potential. Likewise the human capacity of thinking can become an instrument for world domination or can unfold in harmony with its inner nature. In Steiner's view, to give human thought its own "germinating life" ultimately means to allow it to grow and flourish into concentration, meditation, and inspiration. Unfolding and intensifying in this way, thought leads us "directly into the world of spirit"; "People will recognize that the living thought reconfigured in meditation and concentration, leads us to spiritual perception of human nature and the world of spirit."[122] A "living" thought is one that has risen from the "grave" of the physical body, undergoing a "resurrection" in the etheric realm and leading to living perception of the spirit—and thus to the "spiritual revelations" of Michael. It was on this foundation that Rudolf Steiner sought to establish the School of Spiritual Science in Dornach from September 20, 1913, in a way that would enable impulses of renewal for science, art, and religion to become available to earthly civilization. *"Ether being weaves in you…"*[123]

From the beginning, Steiner connected a cosmopolitan peace impulse[124] with the St. John's building in Dornach, later called the Goetheanum. On September 20, 1914, the first anniversary of the laying of the foundation stone, and seven weeks after the decimations of World War I began, he said once again:

> We may celebrate the anniversary of a building that, in the most eminent sense, serves to lead human souls together in harmony across the globe.[125]
>
> If people will take the trouble to study the diverse artistic forms of our building, they will find that…every detail gives expression to the true Christ impulse of uniting all human hearts of the peoples and races of the earth.[126]

Three-and-a-half months previously, on June 1, 1914, he had said something similar in Basel:

> The Christ impulse must penetrate humanity, and truly all people can acknowledge and accept it because the Christ did not appear to one nation only, but, as the sublime being of the sun, belongs to the whole earth and can enter all human souls of any and every nation and religion. May people in great numbers find their way to

such understanding of the Christ impulse, and of the Mystery of Golgotha.[127]

In his lectures on the "preludes" to the Mystery of Golgotha, which Steiner gave immediately before the war, he described in striking terms how the Christ being, together with the Nathan soul, gradually approached the earth to engage with the fortunes of humankind. Through shared self-sacrifice both beings had repeatedly intervened in human evolution in healing ways prior to Golgotha, the Nathan soul always supporting and serving the Christ in this process. The Mystery of Golgotha itself, as Steiner once again emphasized in Pforzheim on March 7, 1914, stood as the "midpoint" and whole meaning of all human evolution on earth. Everything had been prepared in advance for this to occur, was configured to lead up to it; and all evolution since then has been subject to its influence: *"And everything that has happened since then is a gradually progressing influx of the powers of the Mystery of Golgotha into human souls and human hearts."*[128] In 1913 and 1914, Steiner repeatedly and emphatically spoke of the importance of perceiving the presence of the cosmic Christ being (along with the Nathan soul, the pure essence of humanity) in the "spiritual sphere of the earth," and of recognizing how, from there, the Christ "streams through" the hearts and souls of human beings.[129] The Christ presence in this spiritual earth sphere, he said, bears the secret of death and resurrection within it. Christ died at Golgotha in order to share the destiny of earthly humankind:

> He descended from the world in which no death exists into the world of death. Moreover, he—this power—united with the earth. From being a comic power he became a power of the earth. He passed through death

so as to come to life within earth existence, to live in the earthly world.[130]

In 1914 Steiner and Anthroposophy were accused of contradicting the Gospels. The Goetheanum was denigrated as a "gasworks," which Steiner called *"terribly* comical" in the introduction to his Basel lecture on June 1, 1914—decades before the actual "gasworks" and death camps of the twentieth century.

The School of Spiritual Science sought to oppose all contemporary and coming destruction by cultivating the "true progress" of civilization; and the "cry for the spirit" of which Steiner spoke at the laying of its foundation stone on September 20, 1913, testified to the close association of these undertakings, and of Steiner himself, to the Nathan soul[131] and the Christ being. On the eve of the "greatest catastrophe of the twentieth century," and in the era of anti-human, ahrimanic technological materialism, nothing less was involved than the *"continuing survival of the human being."*[132] Passing through pain Christ entered the earth's aura, and as Rudolf Steiner emphasized, humanity must learn to feel connected with this pain of Christ. It must also know that the pain of Christ was working on in "rejuvenating powers" in the earth aura for the future. It was in this spirit that Steiner gave his Christological reflections in the period immediately preceding the war. They were intended not only to help rekindle Christ consciousness in human beings, but at the same time also tap very necessary sources of help, support, and courage.

Writing the concluding chapter of his *Riddles of Philosophy* at the end of August 1914, Steiner said that only body-free awareness was capable of constituting the soul-spiritual core of the human being, and developing, in inner experience, the potential for a "new human nature." After finishing the book and its foreword on September 1, Steiner spoke the same evening in the Berlin branch, and began his lecture with these words:

> My dear friends, I am deeply moved to be with you and speak to you for a little while in these grave times. But our first thoughts must be directed to the dear friends who were so often among us here and who have now been called to the battle field where such fierce conflicts are being waged to decide human destinies and the destinies of nations. Let us rise from our seats for a moment in order to remember these friends in faithful love, sending them our thoughts in which strength may dwell so that they can draw strength in the conditions in which they now stand.
>
> > Spirits, guardians of your souls,
> > May your wings bring
> > The petitioning love of our souls
> > To earthly human beings
> > Entrusted to your protection
> > So that, united with your power
> > Our plea shine out, bring help
> > To the souls it loving seeks.
>
> And to these friends let us call out that the Christ of whom we have so often spoken here may be with them, strengthening them, guarding over them upon the battlefield where the destinies of human beings and nations are now being decided![133]

Steiner also recited this mantric verse, with slight modifications ("sphere-borne human beings / Entrusted to your care...") for the soldiers who had already died, beginning every members' lecture in this way during the war years ("...for combatants on every front, a prayer for help that doubtless issues, and has issued, from nowhere else but here of all places in the world." Emil Leinhas).[134] On September 1, 1914, in Berlin, Steiner also repeated the mantras which he had formulated two weeks previously at a First Aid course in Dornach, and urged the members of the Anthroposophical Society to adopt these in their meditative life. They, too, were expressly connected with the paths of the Nathan soul, the Christ being and a "culture of selflessness":

> As long as *you* feel pain
> That I am spared
> Christ remains unknown
> In his world-working essence;
> For weak the spirit is
> If in a body alone
> It feels only its own suffering.[135]

Notes and References

1. From the introductory words to a lecture Steiner gave in Basel on June 1, 1914. Cf. pp. 3ff. in this volume.
2. Already in an esoteric lesson on October 11, 1913 in Bergen—shortly after the end of the Oslo course on the "Fifth Gospel"—Rudolf Steiner stressed the importance of its contents for "guarding against" a further "increase in egoism" (cf. Rudolf Steiner: CW 266/3, *Esoteric Lessons 1913–1923*, Gt. Barrington: SteinerBooks, 2008).
3. *Rudolf Steiner Über die Schweiz. Äusserungen über die Schweiz aus dem Vortragswerk zusammengestellt und ergänzt durch eine Übersicht der von Rudolf Steiner gehaltenen Vorträge von Hans Hasler.* Dornach 1988, p. 117.
4. First publication of the address of 9.22.1913 in: Roland Halfen, "Dokumente, Erinnerungen, Ansprachen zur Grundsteinlegung des Ersten Goetheanum am 20. September 1913" in: *Archivmagazin,* no. 2, December 2013, p. 96.
5. Ibid., p. 98f.
6. Ibid., p. 99.
7. Ibid., p. 100.
8. Cf. Peter Selg, *Rudolf Steiner: 1861–1925. Life and Work,* vol. 3, Chapter 7, p. 184ff (Gt. Barrington: SteinerBooks, 2015).
9. Cf. Peter Selg: *Rudolf Steiner und die Vorträge über das Fünfte Evangelium.* Dornach 2010, pp. 125ff. [E: *Rudolf Steiner and the Fifth Gospel* (Gt. Barrington: SteinerBooks, 2009).]
10. Rudolf Steiner, *Vorstufen zum Mysterium von Golgotha.* CW 152, Dornach 1990, p. 92. [E: *Approaching the Mystery of Golgotha* (Gt. Barrington: SteinerBooks, 2006).]
11. Cf. Philipp Blom, *Der taumelnde Kontinent. Europa 1900–1914.* Munich 2011.
12. See Peter Selg, *Rudolf Steiner. 1861–1925. Lebens- und Werkgeschichte.* vol. 3, pp. 1589ff. for a summary of views that misperceived and distorted Anthroposophy. [E: *Rudolf Steiner: 1861–1925. Life and Work,* vol. 6 (forthcoming by SteinerBooks).]
13. Rudolf Steiner, *Die Anthroposophie und ihre Gegner.* CW 255b. Dornach 2003, p. 453.

14 Quoted in Lorenzo Ravagli, *Unter Hammer und Hakenkreuz. Der völkisch-nationalsozialistische Kampf gegen die Anthroposophie*. Stuttgart 2004, p. 149.
15 Rudolf Steiner, *Philosophie und Anthroposophie. Gesammelte Aufsätze*. CW 35. Dornach 1984, p. 449f. [E: Fragments of CW 35 appear in *Philosophy and Anthroposophy* (Spring Valley, NY: Mercury Press, 1988).]
16 Ibid., p. 450.
17 In relation to Rudolf Steiner's concept of (conscious) selflessness, cf. Peter Selg, *Die Kultur der Selbstlosigkeit. Rudolf Steiner, das Fünfte Evangelium und das Zeitalter der Extreme*. Dornach 1982, p. 120. [E : *The Culture of Selflessness : Rudolf Steiner, the Fifth Gospel, and the Time of Extremes* (Gt. Barrington: SteinerBooks, 2012).]
18 Rudolf Steiner, *Der Orient im Lichte des Okzidents. Die Kinder des Luzifer und die Brüder Christi*. CW 113. Dornach 1982, p. 120. [E: *The East in the Light of the West*.]
19 Rudolf Steiner, *Vorträge und Kurse über christlich-religiöses Wirken, II. Spirituelles Erkennen—Religiöses Empfinden—Kultisches handeln*. CW 343. Dornach 1993, p. 419.
20 Rudolf Steiner, *Mantrische Sprüche. Seelenübungen*. Band II. CW 268. Dornach 1999, p. 73. [E: *Soul Exercises* (Gt. Barrington: SteinerBooks, 2014).]
21 We now have numerous accounts and analyses of the destructive events of twentieth century history. Cf. among others, the survey by the British historian Eric Hobsbawm (1917–2012) in: *The Age of Extremes: The Short Twentieth Century 1914–1991*, Abacus 1995.
22 Rudolf Steiner, *Die okkulten Grundlagen der Bhagavad Gitas*. CW 146. Dornach, p. 119. [E: *The Bhagavad Gita and the West: The Esoteric Significance of the Bhagavad Gita and Its Relation to the Epistles of Paul* (Gt. Barrington: SteinerBooks, 2006).]
23 Rudolf Steiner, *Vorträge und Kurse über christlich-religiöses Wirken, II. Spirituelles Erkennen—Religiöses Empfinden—Kultisches handeln*. CW 343. Dornach 1993, p. 419.
24 Rudolf Steiner, *Anthroposophische Leitsätze. Der Erkenntnisweg der Anthroposophie—Das Michael-Mysterium*. CW 26. Dornach 1998, p. 110. [E: *Anthroposophical Leading Thoughts: Anthroposophy as a Path of Knowledge: The Michael Mystery* (London: Rudolf Steiner Press, 1999).]
25 For more on Rudolf Steiner's concept of the "'I'-organization" see Peter Selg, *Vom Logos menschlicher Physis. Die Entfaltung einer*

anthroposophischen Humanphysiologie im Werk Rudolf Steiners. vol. II. Dornach 2006, pp. 460ff.

26 Cf. Peter Selg, *Christian Morgenstern. Sein Weg mit Rudolf Steiner.* Stuttgart 2013, p. 283ff; and *Geistige Hilfeleistung. Rudolf Steiner und Christian Morgenstern.* Arlesheim 2014.

27 Rudolf Steiner, *Vortstufen zum Mysterium von Golgotha.* CW 152, p. 164. [E: *Approaching the Mystery of Golgotha* (op. cit.).] In relation to Maria von Strauch-Spetttini and her importance to Marie Steiner-von Sivers, Rudolf Steiner, and the mystery plays, see Hella Wiesberger, *Marie Steiner-von Sivers—ein Leben für die Anthroposophie.* Dornach 1988, p. 45ff; Peter Selg, *Marie Steiner Steiner-von Sivers. Aufbau und Zukunft des Werkes von Rudolf Steiner.* Dornach 2006, p. 74ff and Andreas Neider, *Christus-Impuls und Rosenkreuzertum. Rudolf Steiners Weg zum Fünften Evangelium.* Stuttgart 2011, pp. 22ff.

28 Quoted in Marie Steiner (ed.), *Die Sehnsucht der Seelen nach Geist. Ein Zeichen der Zeit. Worte Rudolf Steiners am ersten Jahrestag der Grundsteinlegung des Goetheanum in Dornach am 20. September 1914.* Dornach 1938, p. 20f.

29 Rudolf Steiner, *Die Verbindung zwischen Lebenden und Toten.* CW 168. Dornach 1995, p. 214. [E: *Spiritual Research, Methods and Results* (Garber, 1981).]

30 In this context see, among others, Peter Selg, "'Es walten die Übel.' Die Nichtweiterführung der Vorträge." In: *Rudolf Steiner und die Vorträge über das Fünfte Evangelium,* pp. 123ff. [E: *Rudolf Steiner and the Fifth Gospel* (op. cit.).] Andrei Belyi, Friedrich Rittelmeyer and others have written about how Rudolf Steiner's lectures on the intimate context of the "Fifth Gospel" were not met with the reticent, serious, and sensitive reception they would have required. Rudolf Steiner had emphatically asked for both an active and "discreet" reception of these accounts in anthroposophic branch meetings; but as early as September 1909, when he first spoke in detail about the Luke Jesus child, and thus about the Nathan soul, no heed whatever was paid to this request. (Steiner said on 11.4.1913 in Berlin that his reflections at the time had been "rendered ridiculous ... by incautious chatter" although they should by rights be "sacred matters" for anthroposophists. See *Aus der Akasha-Forschung. Das Fünfte Evangelium.* CW 148, p. 135. [E: *The Fifth Gospel: From the Akashic Record* (London: Rudolf Steiner Press, 1995).]) In his reminiscences, Friedrich Rittelmeyer mentioned that at the time an "appallingly distorted picture" of Steiner was going the rounds of the illustrated newspapers, with

the caption, "The Fifth Evangelist" (*Meine Lebensbegegnung mit Rudolf Steiner*. Stuttgart 1983, p. 63 [E: *Rudolf Steiner Enters My Life* (Edinburgh: Floris Books, 2013).]). The last lecture for members which Rudolf Steiner gave on the "Fifth Gospel" (in which he also gave an account of the "preludes" to the Mystery of Golgotha) on May 27, 1914 in Paris—just five days before the Basel lecture—was attended by three note-taking journalists from big French daily newspapers. Rudolf Steiner was only alerted to their presence at the end of the lecture. In the correspondence preceding his lecture he had asked that care be taken to protect this members-only lecture in the French capital (cf. Irene Diet, *Jules und Alice Sauerwein und der Kampf um die Anthroposophie in Frankreich*. Zeist 1998, p. 147). Clearly this did not happen. When informed of the presence of the journalists he responded accordingly. Pieter de Haan, who attended this lecture in Paris and heard subsequent comments by Steiner, wrote decades later of his memory of this: "For forty minutes at least he expressed his indignation, doing so with self-control but with great insistence and intensity. He simply went on and on. He launched again and again into expression of his dismay. He hammered his displeasure deep into our souls. His words were of penetrating power and controlled force, and left us standing there in perplexity. This revealed an aspect of his nature which most of us were unaware of. Fortunately however, we succeeded in preventing publication of the newspaper articles in question." (Pieter de Hahn, "Erinnerungen an Rudolf Steiner." Quoted in Irene Diet, op. cit., p. 147). For many years Steiner refused to give permission for an internal (manuscript) printing of his Basel cycle on the Gospel of St. Luke about the Luke Jesus child (cf. Irene Diet, *Ist die "Rudolf Steiner Gesamtausgabe" ein Werk Rudolf Steiners? Eine historische Studie*. Dietlikon 2013, pp. 89ff.).

31   In relation to the two addresses (one in the trench and one beside it) cf. Erika von Baravalle (ed.), *Rudolf Steiners Grundsteinlegung am 20. September 1913*. Arlesheim 2013, pp. 233ff.; Roland Halfen, "Dokumente, Erinnerungen, Ansprachen zur Grundsteinlegung des Ersten Goetheanum am 20. September 1913" in, *Archivmagazin*, no. 2, December 2013, pp. 84ff.; and Rudolf Grosse, *Die Weihnachtstagung als Zeitenwende und die Grundsteinlegung des ersten Goetheanum*. Dornach 2013, pp. 31ff. [E: *The Christmas Foundation* (Steiner Book Centre, 1984).]

32   Cf. Peter Selg, *Grundstein zur Zukunft. Vom Schicksal der Michael-Gemeinschaft*. Arlesheim 2013, pp. 13ff. [E: *The Destiny*

of the Michael Community: Foundation Stone for the Future (Gt. Barrington: SteinerBooks, 2014).]

33 Rudolf Steiner, *Aus der Akasha-Forschung. Das Fünfte Evangelium.* CW 148. Dornach 1992, p. 219. [E: *The Fifth Gospel: From the Akashic Record* (op. cit.).]

34 Cf. Rudolf Steiner, *Das Lukas-Evangelium.* CW 114. [E: *According to Luke: The Gospel of Compassion and Love Revealed* (Gt. Barrington: Anthroposophic Press, 2001).]

35 Cf. Hella Krause Zimmer, "Wann began Rudolf Steiner über die zwei Jesusknaben zu sprechen und wie klangen seine Darstellungen des Themas vorher?" In, *Mitteilungen aus der anthroposophischen Arbeit in Deutschland.* No. 163, Easter 1988, p. 28–41.

36 Rudolf Steiner, *Vorstufen zum Mysterium von Golgotha.* CW 152, p. 93. [E: *Approaching the Mystery of Golgotha* (op. cit.).]

37 Genesis I,26. For a discussion of "essence" and "image" in relation to the Nathan soul and the Zarathustra "I," see the accounts by Sergei O. Prokofieff, *The First Class of the Michael School and Its Christological Foundations* (Dornach, 2012), pp. 332ff.

38 Rudolf Steiner, *Christus und die geistige Welt. Von der Suche nach dem heiligen Gral.* CW 149. Dornach 2004, p. 61. [E: *Christ and the Spiritual World: The Search for the Holy Grail* (London: Rudolf Steiner Press, 2008).]

39 Rudolf Steiner, *Vorstufen zum Mysterium von Golgotha.* CW 152, p. 102. [E: *Approaching the Mystery of Golgotha* (op. cit.).]

40 In relation to this "enlargement" that also affected and transformed the corporeality of Jesus, Rudolf Steiner said in his Karlsruhe course, *From Jesus to Christ*: "Once the inmost quality of human nature had arisen with the most intensive powers of love and compassion through the fact that a pure human essence was preserved until the birth of the Nathan Jesus, and the astral body then permeated itself with the powers of Gautama Buddha—and thus once there was present in the Nathan Jesus what we can call 'the inmost inwardness' of the human being—there connected with this corporeality at the age of twelve the human individuality who, among all human individualities, had gazed most clearly and profoundly into the spirituality of the cosmos. By virtue of this, the instruments of the Nathan Jesus were transformed so that they became able to absorb the essence of Christ from the macrocosm. If the individuality of Zarathustra had not fully penetrated this corporeality by the age of 30, his eyes would not have been capable of enduring the substance of Christ from his thirtieth year until the Mystery of Golgotha, his hands would not have been

capable of penetration by the substance of Christ in his thirtieth year. To be able to absorb the Christ, this bodily nature had as it were to be prepared and enlarged through the individuality of Zarathustra." (Rudolf Steiner, *Von Jesus zu Christus*. CW 131. Dornach 1988, p. 184 [E: *From Jesus to Christ* (London: Rudolf Steiner Press, 2005.]).

41 Rudolf Steiner, *Aus der Akasha-Forschung. Das Fünfte Evangelium*. CW 148, p. 255. [E: *The Fifth Gospel: From the Akashic Record* (op. cit.).]
42 Ibid., p. 134.
43 Ibid., p. 66.
44 Ibid., p. 71.
45 Ibid., p. 298.
46 Ibid., p. 310.
47 Ibid., p. 310 f.
48 (In the German version, the word *straitened* is rendered as "fearful.") See Rudolf Frieling, "Von der Jordantaufe zur Schädelstätte" in, *Gesammelte Schriften zum Alten und Neuen Testament,* vol. III. Stuttgart 1982, p. 28 [E: *New Testament Studies* (Edinburgh: Floris, 1994), *Old Testament Studies* (ibid., 2015)]; and Peter Selg, *Das Ereignis der Jordantaufe. Epiphanaias im Urchristentum und in der Anthroposophie Rudolf Steiners*. Stuttgart 2008, pp. 55ff. ("Der Vollzug der Jordantaufe").
49 Cf. Sergei O. Prokofieff: *The Mystery of the Resurrection in the Light of Anthroposophy* (London: Temple Lodge, 2010).
50 Rudolf Steiner, *Aus der Akasha-Forschung. Das Fünfte Evangelium*. CW 148, p. 278. [E: *The Fifth Gospel: From the Akashic Record* (op. cit.).]
51 Ibid., p. 218.
52 Ibid., p. 324.
53 See the testimonies in Peter Selg, *Rudolf Steiner und die Vorträge über das Fünfte Evangelium,* pp. 15ff. and 40ff. in relation to the astonishment of his audience and the dramatic style in which the cycle began. [E: *Rudolf Steiner and the Fifth Gospel* (op. cit.).]
54 Following the lecture in Leipzig, Rudolf Steiner also named the Nathan being very directly on March 5, 1914 in Stuttgart, whereas in all subsequent lectures (in Pforzheim, Munich, Paris, and Basel) he mostly spoke of an "angel" or "archangel" being, or of an "angel-" or "archangel-type" being (cf. *Vorstufen zum Mysterium* von Golgotha. CW 152, for example p. 102 f./118/123/135/154/161 [E: *Approaching the Mystery of Golgotha* (op. cit.)]); in Pforzheim and Munich, however, it was made clear

Notes and References

at least that the later Nathan Jesus child is identical with this "angel" or "archangel" being (cf. pp. 102ff. and 121ff.). We can only imagine why, in most places, Rudolf Steiner scarcely mentioned the Nathan being by name, or did not mention him at all, but only indirectly referred to him. See also note 30 above.

55 See Rudolf Steiner, *Anthroposophische Leitsätze. Der Erkenntnisweg der Anthroposophie—Das Michael-Mysterium*. CW 26. Dornach 1998, pp. 197ff. [E: *Anthroposophical Leading Thoughts: Anthroposophy as a Path of Knowledge: The Michael Mystery* (op. cit.).]

56 Rudolf Steiner, *Vorstufen zum Mysterium von Golgotha*. CW 152, p. 94. [E: *Approaching the Mystery of Golgotha* (op. cit.).]

57 Rudolf Steiner, *Christus und die geistige Welt. Von der Suche nach dem heiligen Gral*. CW 149, p. 49. [E: *Christ and the Spiritual World: The Search for the Holy Grail* (op. cit.).]

58 Rudolf Steiner, *Aus der Akasha-Forschung. Das Fünfte Evangelium*. CW 148, p. 76. [E: *The Fifth Gospel: From the Akashic Record* (op. cit.).]

59 Rudolf Steiner, *Christus und die geistige Welt. Von der Suche nach dem heiligen Gral*. CW 149, p. 49. [E: *Christ and the Spiritual World: The Search for the Holy Grail* (op. cit.).]

60 Sergei O. Prokofieff, "The Three Supersensible Deeds of the Nathan Soul," pp. 39ff; in *The Cycle of the Year as a Path of Initiation Leading to an Experience of the Christ Being* (London: Temple Lodge, [1991] 2014). With this book on Christology, which he finished writing in 1985 (Stuttgart 1986), Sergei O. Prokofieff became the first author since Rudolf Steiner to engage extensively with the theme of the Nathan soul. Despite the outstanding importance of this for an understanding of the Mystery of Golgotha, it had for many decades remained in the background of anthroposophical studies, and even of anthroposophical awareness.

61 Rudolf Steiner, *Vorstufen zum Mysterium von Golgotha*. CW 152, p. 135. [E: *Approaching the Mystery of Golgotha* (op. cit.).]

62 Rudolf Steiner, *Christus und die geistige Welt. Von der Suche nach dem heiligen Gral*. CW 149, p. 50. [E: *Christ and the Spiritual World: The Search for the Holy Grail* (op. cit.).]

63 Rudolf Steiner, *Vorstufen zum Mysterium von Golgotha*. CW 152, p. 122. [E: *Approaching the Mystery of Golgotha* (op. cit.).]

64 Ibid., p. 106.

65 According to Sergei O. Prokofieff's account, which is based on a survey of various comments by Rudolf Steiner, also relating to

general Anthroposophy and cosmology, and thorough meditative engagement with this material, the process occurring within the sun sphere was such that the Nathan soul ascended to the loftiest region of the sun, "where the sun acts as a fixed star among fixed stars, and from where it is possible to reach the primordial sources of the spiritual currents that emanate from the twelve world spheres of the zodiac. In permeating his whole being with the twelve powers of the zodiac—whose interplay not only forms the twelve sense organs but also the human being's physical form—the Nathan soul was, in this sphere, able to sacrifice his own etheric being to the sun spirit of Christ. Thanks to this occurrence, the archetypal 'etheric human form' arose in the lower regions of the world of spirit" (*The Cycle of the Year as a Path of Initiation Leading to an Experience of the Christ Being*, pp. 40–41 [op. cit.]).

66 Rudolf Steiner, *Vorstufen zum Mysterium von Golgotha*. CW 152, p. 106. [E: *Approaching the Mystery of Golgotha* (op. cit.).]

67 Ibid., p. 106f.

68 Rudolf Steiner, *Christus und die geistige Welt. Von der Suche nach dem heiligen Gral*. CW 149, p. 51. [E: *Christ and the Spiritual World: The Search for the Holy Grail* (op. cit.).]

69 Sergei O. Prokofieff wrote as follows about this whole process of sacrifice within the planetary sphere: "The Nathan soul had to absorb the powers of all seven planets in order to be able then to sacrifice his whole being once again to the sublime sun spirit Christ and for a second time become the bearer of Christ in the cosmos, the heavenly Christophorus. Because of this it became possible for the Christ to transform the powers of the separate planets which the Nathan soul had gathered together so that they were able to lend order and harmony to the etheric body, and through it bring healing to the seven chief planets" (Sergei O. Prokofieff, *The Cycle of the Year as a Path of Initiation Leading to an Experience of the Christ Being*, p. 42 [op. cit.]).

70 Rudolf Steiner, *Christus und die geistige Welt. Von der Suche nach dem heiligen Gral*. CW 149, p. 52f. [E: *Christ and the Spiritual World: The Search for the Holy Grail* (op. cit.).]

71 Rudolf Steiner, *Vorstufen zum Mysterium von Golgotha*. CW 152, p. 95. [E: *Approaching the Mystery of Golgotha* (op. cit.).]

72 Ibid., p. 109f.; concerning the connection between the Nathan soul and the human being's individual capacity for speech and thinking, see also Rudolf Steiner's esoteric lesson on 12.7.1909 in, *Aus den Inhalten der esoterischen Stunden*. CW 266a. Dornach

2007, p. 549. [E: *Esoteric Lessons 1904–1914* (Gt. Barrington: SteinerBooks, 2006).] See also Sergei O. Prokofieff, *The First Class of the Michael School and Its Christological Foundations*, pp. 364ff (op. cit.).

73 Rudolf Steiner, *From Jesus to Christ* (op. cit.). CW 131. Concerning this course and the spiritual-scientific dimension of the resurrection body, see Sergei O. Prokofieff, *The Mystery of the Resurrection in the Light of Anthroposophy* (London: Temple Lodge, 2010).

74 Rudolf Steiner, *Die Rätsel der Philosophie in ihrer Geschichte als Umriss dargestellt*. CW 18. Dornach 1985, pp. 35ff. [E: *The Riddles of Philosophy* (Gt. Barrington: SteinerBooks, 2009).]

75 Rudolf Steiner, *Vorstufen zum Mysterium von Golgotha*. CW 152, p. 66. [E: *Approaching the Mystery of Golgotha* (op. cit.).]

76 Rudolf Steiner, *Christus und die geistige Welt. Von der Suche nach dem heiligen Gral*. CW 149, p. 14f. [E: *Christ and the Spiritual World: The Search for the Holy Grail* (op. cit.).]

77 Ibid., p. 13.

78 Ibid., p. 39.

79 Rudolf Steiner, *Aus der Akasha-Forschung. Das Fünfte Evangelium*. CW 148, p. 198. [E: *The Fifth Gospel: From the Akashic Record* (op. cit.).]

80 Rudolf Steiner, *Geisteswissenschaft als Lebensgut*. CW 63. Dornach 1986, p. 209.

81 Rudolf Steiner, *Vorstufen zum Mysterium von Golgotha*. CW 152, p. 138. [E: *Approaching the Mystery of Golgotha* (op. cit.).]

82 Ibid., p. 125.

83 Ibid., p. 139.

84 Rudolf Steiner, *Christus und die geistige Welt. Von der Suche nach dem heiligen Gral*. CW 149, p. 40; author's emphasis. [E: *Christ and the Spiritual World: The Search for the Holy Grail* (op. cit.).]

85 Rudolf Steiner, *Vorstufen zum Mysterium von Golgotha*. CW 152, p. 97. [E: *Approaching the Mystery of Golgotha* (op. cit.).]

86 Ibid., p. 126; author's emphasis.

87 See, for instance, Markus Osterrieder, "Im 'okkulten Untergrund'" in, *Welt im Umbruch. Nationalitätsfrage, Ordnungspläne und Rudolf Steiner's Haltung im Ersten Weltkrieg*. Stuttgart 2014, p. 267–496.

88 Rudolf Steiner, *Christus und die geistige Welt. Von der Suche nach dem heiligen Gral*. CW 149, p. 41. [E: *Christ and the Spiritual World: The Search for the Holy Grail* (op. cit.).]

89   Cf. Peter Selg, *Rudolf Steiner und die Vorträge über das Fünfte Evangelium*, p. 60f. [E: *Rudolf Steiner and the Fifth Gospel* (Gt. Barrington: SteinerBooks, 2009).]
90   Rudolf Steiner, *Vorstufen zum Mysterium von Golgotha.* CW 152, p. 112. [E: *Approaching the Mystery of Golgotha* (op. cit.).]
91   Ibid., p. 113.
92   Cf. Peter Selg, *Grundstein zur Zukunft. Vom Schicksal der Michael-Gemeinschaft*, pp. 37ff. [E: *The Destiny of the Michael Community: Foundation Stone for the Future* (op. cit.).]
93   See Rudolf Steiner, *Anthroposophische Leitsätze. Der Erkenntnisweg der Anthroposophie—Das Michael-Mysterium.* CW 26, p. 79. [E: *Anthroposophical Leading Thoughts: Anthroposophy as a Path of Knowledge: The Michael Mystery* (op. cit.).]
94   Ibid., p. 83.
95   Ibid., p. 80.
96   "By 1843/44 everything had really already been decided as far as materialism is concerned. Everything else was, basically, the effect of this, and will continue to be so. But the point of time at the beginning of the 1840s is of huge significance for what happened to European civilization and its American appendage, since at that time the influx of ahrimanic powers into human affairs was enormously intense. We can say that after 1843/44 worse things transpired; and yet, you see, this was only apparently so. You need only realize that Ahriman is cleverer than human beings. It was Ahriman who was acting, largely, in 1843/44. He arranged things as his intelligence dictates. This was the nadir or if you like the culmination of the materialistic path. After this human beings continued industriously in this vein, and though what arose as they did so assumed far uglier proportions, it was not as dire for overall human evolution. If we consider this from a spiritual perspective, it is the aftereffect of what was projected by Ahriman at the beginning of the 1840s." Rudolf Steiner, *The Book of Revelation and the Work of the Priest*, CW 346, p. 178f. (London: Rudolf Steiner Press, 1998)]. Concerning the consequences of these occurrences, see for instance Peter Selg, "Die geistige Dimension des Menschen? Zur Entwicklung der medizinischen Anthropologie im 20. Jahrhundert" in, Peter Heusser/Peter Selg, *Das Leib-Seele Problem. Zur Entwicklung eines geistgemässen Menschenbildes in der Medizin des 20. Jahrhunderts.* Arlesheim 2011, pp. 35ff.
97   Rudolf Steiner, *Vorstufen zum Mysterium von Golgotha.* CW 152, p. 70. [E: *Approaching the Mystery of Golgotha* (op. cit.).]

98   Sergei O. Prokofieff, "Die Menschheitsaufgabe der nathanischen Seele" in, *Gemeinschaftsbildung im Lichte Michaels.* Ed. Richard Steel. Dornach 2010, p. 52. [E: "The Task of the Nathan Soul for Humanity." In: R. Steele (ed.): *Communities for Tomorrow,* (Edinburgh: Floris Books, 2011).

99   Rudolf Steiner, *Vorstufen zum Mysterium von Golgotha.* CW 152, p.71f. [E: *Approaching the Mystery of Golgotha* (op. cit.).]

100   Ibid., p. 46. In my view, the second volume of Sergei O. Prokofieff's studies on the Michael School represents an outstanding and exemplary highpoint of such consciousness. The book is entitled, *Der esoterische Weg durch die neunzehn Klassenstunden im Lichte des übersinnlichen Mysteriums von Golgotha und des Fünften Evangeliums.* Dornach 2014. (English edition forthcoming.)

101   Andreas Neider, *Michael und die Apokalypse des 20. Jahrhunderts. Das Jahr 1913 im Lebensgang Rudolf Steiners.* Stuttgart 2013, p. 32f.

102   Rudolf Steiner, *Aus der Akasha-Forschung. Das Fünfte Evangelium.* CW 148, p. 310. [E: *The Fifth Gospel: From the Akashic Record* (op. cit.).] See also Sergei O. Prokofieff: *The Guardian of the Threshold and the Philosophy of Freedom* (London: Temple Lodge, 2011).

103   See Peter Selg, *Rudolf Steiner, Life and Work,* vol. 3 (Gt. Barrington: SteinerBooks 2015), pp. 168ff.

104   "But what was ... the first Goetheanum building? What first became visible through it? It was the Christ consciousness reawakening in the lectures on the Gospels. The building was intended to render this reawakening consciousness visible again for the first time, just as it had been offered to human beings a year before in the Soul Calendar, in 1912/13, as meditation material for them to engage with." (Andreas Neider, *Michael und die Apokalypse des 20. Jahrhunderts. Das Jahr 1913 im Lebensgang Rudolf Steiners,* p. 38). See also Sergei O. Prokofieff / Peter Selg, *The Creative Power of Anthroposophical Christology* (Gt. Barrington: SteinerBooks, 2012), Part 2: *The First Goetheanum and Its Christological Foundations,* pp. 75ff.

105   See Rudolf Steiner, *Anthroposophische Leitsätze. Der Erkenntnisweg der Anthroposophie—Das Michael-Mysterium.* CW 26, p. 152/4. [E: *Anthroposophical Leading Thoughts: Anthroposophy as a Path of Knowledge: The Michael Mystery* (op. cit.).]

106 Concerning Michael's importance for the Nathan being—safeguarding him from a premature incarnation, protecting him in his three deeds of sacrifice before the advent of Christ, and during the events at the time of Christ and in the nineteenth century—cf. Sergei O. Prokofieff, *The Cycle of the Year as a Path of Initiation Leading to an Experience of the Christ Being* (op. cit.), pp. 45ff. Also Andreas Neider, *Michael und die Apokalypse des 20. Jahrhunderts. Das Jahr 1913 im Lebensgang Rudolf Steiners*, pp. 40ff.

107 See Peter Selg, "Rudolf Steiner, the Fifth Gospel, and Christ's Reappearance in the Etheric" in Sergei O. Prokofieff / Peter Selg, *The Creative Power of Anthroposophical Christology* (op. cit.), pp. 145ff.

108 Rudolf Steiner, *Vorstufen zum Mysterium von Golgotha*. CW 152, p. 91. [E: *Approaching the Mystery of Golgotha* (op. cit.).]

109 Ibid., p. 45.

110 Ibid., p. 118.

111 Concerning the Nathan's soul involvement in the reappearance of Christ in the etheric, and later in still loftier spiritual regions, see Sergei O. Prokofieff, "Rudolf Steiner and the Influence of the Nathan Soul" in, *And the Earth Becomes a Sun* (Stourbridge: Wynstones, 2014), pp. 405ff. Also, Sergei O. Prokofieff: *The Appearance of Christ in The Etheric: Spiritual-Scientific Aspects of the Second Coming* (London: Temple Lodge 2012).

112 Rudolf Steiner, *Wahrspruchworte*. CW 40. Dornach 2005, p. 97. [E: *Verses and Meditations* (London: Rudolf Steiner Press, 2004).]

113 Rudolf Steiner, *Vorstufen zum Mysterium von Golgotha*. CW 152, p. 43. [E: *Approaching the Mystery of Golgotha* (op. cit.).]

114 Ibid., p. 44.

115 Ibid., p. 52.

116 Ibid.

117 Concerning the content and anthroposophic background to the "reversed" Lord's Prayer in the "Fifth Gospel," see Peter Selg, *Rudolf Steiner und die Vorträge über das Fünfte Evangelium*, p. 60f. [E: *Rudolf Steiner and the Fifth Gospel* (op. cit.).]

118 Rudolf Steiner, *Aus der Akasha-Forschung. Das Fünfte Evangelium*. CW 148, p. 251. [E: *The Fifth Gospel: From the Akashic Record* (op. cit.).]

119 Ibid., p. 92.

120 According to Christoph Lindenberg, Rudolf Steiner wrote the "Outline perspective on Anthroposophy" from August 29–31, 1914 in Berlin. (*Rudolf Steiner. Eine Chronik. 1861–1925*. Stuttgart 1988, p. 354.)

Notes and References

121 Cf. Peter Selg, *Rudolf Steiner: 1861–1925. Lebens- und Werkgeschichte*. vol. 2, pp. 915ff. [E: *Rudolf Steiner: 1861–1925. Life and Work*. vol. 4 (translation forthcoming from SteinerBooks).]
122 Rudolf Steiner, *Vorstufen zum Mysterium von Golgotha*. CW 152, p. 131. [E: *Approaching the Mystery of Golgotha* (op. cit.).]
123 Rudolf Steiner, *Esoterische Unterweisungen für die erste Klasse der Freien Hochschule für Geisteswissenschaft am Goetheanum 1924*, vol. 1. CW 270a. Dornach 2008, p. 51.
124 Cf. Peter Selg, *Rudolf Steiner: 1861–1925. Lebens- und Werkgeschichte*. vol. 2, pp. 912ff. [E: *Rudolf Steiner: 1861–1925. Life and Work*, vol. 4 (translation forthcoming from SteinerBooks).]
125 Rudolf Steiner, *Schicksalszeichen auf dem Entwickelungswege der Anthroposophischen Gesellschaft*. Dornach 1943, p. 37.
126 Ibid.
127 Rudolf Steiner, *Vorstufen zum Mysterium von Golgotha*. CW 152, p. 166. [E: *Approaching the Mystery of Golgotha* (op. cit.).]
128 Ibid., p. 103.
129 Ibid., p. 102.
130 Ibid., p. 71.
131 Cf. for example Sergei O. Prokofieff, "Rudolf Steiner and the Influence of the Nathan Soul" in, *And the Earth Becomes a Sun* (op. cit.), pp. 405ff. Also, Sergei O. Prokofieff, "The Mystery of the Resurrection in the Light of the Fifth Gospel." In, Sergei O. Prokofieff / Peter Selg, *The Creative Power of Anthroposophical Christology* (op. cit.), pp. 173ff.
132 Rudolf Steiner, *Vorträge und Kurse über christlich-religiöses Wirken, II. Spirituelles Erkennen—Religiöses Empfinden—Kultisches handeln*. CW 343, p. 511.
133 Rudolf Steiner, *Menschenschicksale und Völkerschicksale*. CW 157. Dornach 1981, p. 15. [E: Rudolf Steiner, *The Destinies of Individuals and of Nations*, (London: Rudolf Steiner Press, 1987).
134 Emil Leinhas, *Aus der Arbeit mit Rudolf Steiner*. Basel 1950, p. 26. Concerning Rudolf Steiner's situation and conduct during the years of World War I, see Peter Selg, *Rudolf Steiner 1861–1925. Lebens- und Werkgeschichte*. vol. 2, p. 887–1267. [E: *Rudolf Steiner: 1861–1925. Life and Work*, vol. 4 (translation forthcoming from SteinerBooks).]
135 Rudolf Steiner, *Mantrische Sprüche. Seelenübungen*. Band II. CW 268, p. 195. [E: *Soul Exercises* (op. cit.).]

Books in English Translation by Peter Selg

ON RUDOLF STEINER

Rudolf Steiner: Life and Work: (1890–1900): Weimar and Berlin, vol. 2 of 7 (2014)

Rudolf Steiner: Life and Work: (1861–1890): Childhood, Youth, and Study Years, vols. 1–3 of 7 (2014–2015)

Rudolf Steiner and Christian Rosenkreutz (2012)

Rudolf Steiner as a Spiritual Teacher: From Recollections of Those Who Knew Him (2010)

ON CHRISTOLOGY

The Lord's Prayer and Rudolf Steiner: A Study of His Insights into the Archetypal Prayer of Christianity (2014)

The Creative Power of Anthroposophical Christology: An Outline of Occult Science · The First Goetheanum · The Fifth Gospel · The Christmas Conference (with Sergei O. Prokofieff) (2012)

Christ and the Disciples: The Destiny of an Inner Community (2012)

The Figure of Christ: Rudolf Steiner and the Spiritual Intention behind the Goetheanum's Central Work of Art (2009)

Rudolf Steiner and the Fifth Gospel: Insights into a New Understanding of the Christ Mystery (2010)

Seeing Christ in Sickness and Healing (2005)

On General Anthroposophy

The Destiny of the Michael Community: Foundation Stone for the Future (2014)

Spiritual Resistance: Ita Wegman 1933–1935 (2014)

The Last Three Years: Ita Wegman in Ascona, 1940–1943 (2014)

From Gurs to Auschwitz: The Inner Journey of Maria Krehbiel-Darmstädter (2013)

Crisis in the Anthroposophical Society: And Pathways to the Future (2013); with Sergei O. Prokofieff

Rudolf Steiner's Foundation Stone Meditation: And the Destruction of the Twentieth Century (2013)

The Culture of Selflessness: Rudolf Steiner, the Fifth Gospel, and the Time of Extremes (2012)

The Mystery of the Heart: The Sacramental Physiology of the Heart in Aristotle, Thomas Aquinas, and Rudolf Steiner (2012)

Rudolf Steiner and the School for Spiritual Science: The Foundation of the "First Class" (2012)

Rudolf Steiner's Intentions for the Anthroposophical Society: The Executive Council, the School for Spiritual Science, and the Sections (2011)

The Fundamental Social Law: Rudolf Steiner on the Work of the Individual and the Spirit of Community (2011)

The Path of the Soul after Death: The Community of the Living and the Dead as Witnessed by Rudolf Steiner in his Eulogies and Farewell Addresses (2011)

The Agriculture Course, Koberwitz, Whitsun 1924: Rudolf Steiner and the Beginnings of Biodynamics (2010)

Books in English Translation by Peter Selg

On Anthroposophical Medicine and Curative Education

Honoring Life: Medical Ethics and Physician-Assisted Suicide (2014); with Sergei O. Prokofieff

I Am for Going Ahead: Ita Wegman's Work for the Social Ideals of Anthroposophy (2012)

The Child with Special Needs: Letters and Essays on Curative Education (Ed.) (2009)

Ita Wegman and Karl König: Letters and Documents (2008)

Karl König's Path to Anthroposophy (2008)

Karl König: My Task: Autobiography and Biographies (Ed.) (2008)

On Child Development and Waldorf Education

I Am Different from You: How Children Experience Themselves and the World in the Middle of Childhood (2011)

Unbornness: Human Pre-existence and the Journey toward Birth (2010)

The Essence of Waldorf Education (2010)

The Therapeutic Eye: How Rudolf Steiner Observed Children (2008)

A Grand Metamorphosis: Contributions to the Spiritual-Scientific Anthropology and Education of Adolescents (2008)

Ita Wegman Institute
for Basic Research into Anthroposophy

Pfeffinger Weg 1a, ch 4144 Arlesheim, Switzerland
www.wegmaninstitut.ch
e-mail: sekretariat@wegmaninstitut.ch

The Ita Wegman Institute for Basic Research into Anthroposophy is a non-profit research and teaching organization. It undertakes basic research into the lifework of Dr. Rudolf Steiner (1861–1925) and the application of Anthroposophy in specific areas of life, especially medicine, education, and curative education. Work carried out by the Institute is supported by a number of foundations and organizations and an international group of friends and supporters. The Director of the Institute is Prof. Dr. Peter Selg.

www.ingramcontent.com/pod-product-compliance
Lightning Source LLC
Chambersburg PA
CBHW020944090426
42736CB00010B/1256